A Directory of Library and Information Retrieval Software for Microcomputers

3rd edition

ACKNOWLEDGEMENTS

The authors wish to thank the European Host Organisation, in particular Roland Haber and Peter Cornelius, for all their work in creating the database IR-SOFT from which this directory is printed and in editing and amending the text for output in printed form. Thanks are also due to the many individuals who have helped us to locate new packages or updated us on existing entries.

Contents

INTRODUCTION	vii
SOME NOTES ON SOFTWARE SELECTION	ix
ALPHABETICAL LIST OF SOFTWARE PACKAGES	1
INDEXES	53
FUNCTION INDEX	53
HARDWARE INDEX	60
SUPPLIER INDEX	69

Introduction

This updated directory aims to provide a single source of details of microcomputer software for library and information work. Software which is specifically designed to provide the following functions is included:

Acquisitions, including: printed and online orders, receipts, fund accounting and stock preparation

Administration, including: budgets and financial control, statistics and management information

Archive control

Audio visual control, including: catalogues and software and hardware lending

Catalogues, including: cards, printed, COM and online catalogues, links to union/co-operative catalogues and retrospective conversion

Circulation control, including: borrower registration, control of issue and return, overdue notices and fines

Information retrieval from microcomputer databases, using data from hosts' database subsets on disk or inhouse data. This category excludes most general purpose filing systems, concentrating rather on text retrieval software and other IR packages written with the librarian/information specialist in mind

Information retrieval from online hosts (online search aids) including: autologon, stored passwords and search strategies, downloading and access to specific hosts (whilst many standard communications packages can be used, the authors' aim was to restrict the entries to software designed specifically for online searching or communications software in common use by libraries)

Indexes and thesaurus control

Interlibrary loans

Reference management, for example: abstracts, accessions lists, bibliographies, bulletins and reading lists

Serials control, including: subscriptions, receipt, routing, financial control and union lists

User education: software designed specifically for library user education or which may be adapted

Viewdata: packages to assist in accessing remote systems or to create an inhouse viewdata system

Many libraries have successfully automated their libraries using "business" software, such as word processing, spreadsheet, database management and file management systems. Such software is excluded because information about it is readily available in major software directories.

Software developed or adapted by library schools for use in their teaching programs is also excluded. Details of such software, available in the UK, may be traced through CALLISTO, a bibliography available from:

Joan Day, School of Librarianship and Information Studies, Newcastle Polytechnic, Lipman Building, Sandyford Road, Newcastle upon Tyne, NE1 8ST
Telephone: 0632 612181 extension 12

Although some CD-ROM databases are included, these are not comprehensive. For further details enquirers should use:

RASDALL, Mark (ed.)
The International Directory of Information
Products on CD ROM 1986/7
ISBN: 0-946291-160

Details of software from all around the world are included, but no attempt has been made to be comprehensive in the coverage of software originating outside the UK.

The details provided for each package are culled from trade literature, the professional press and the supplier, and the validity and accuracy of the information cannot be guaranteed. The purpose of the directory is as a guide to potentially suitable software, and it is recommended that further information is sought from the supplier.

The entries, which are in alphabetical order of package name, are indexed by:

— the supplier

— the application(s) the software has been designed to perform

— the hardware which is required to run the package, or if no specific model is required, the operating system

and contain the following details:

— name

— supplier, address and telephone number

— operating system

— hardware

— price and currency

— a brief note about the item

— reference to relevent articles in the literature

— application index terms

In view of the constantly changing software marketplace, it is intended to update this directory annually or as major changes dictate.

Notes on software selection

Faced with the bewildering array of software that is currently available, the librarian or information manager needs to weigh up several factors in order to choose a package suitable for his/her needs. Some points which should be considered are outlined here as a brief guide.

Analysing the system to be automated is the first stage. It is important to:

— ensure that automation is the best or only solution to the problem.

— define the objective of automation (i.e. to save time, save money or improve the service).

— analyse the functions required and rank them in order of importance (for example, rapid searching may be important or ease of input and editing of data).

— identify the data elements (fields) needed.

— calculate the maximum size of fields and records (the maximum record is the **sum** of all the maximum fields). When calculating size, spaces, punctuation, letters and numbers should all be counted.

— estimate the total storage capacity required. To do this, multiply the number of characters in the records by the estimated number of records, allowing for growth. The record size should be the **average** number of characters where variable fields are to be used, the **maximum** for fixed fields.

Having defined the system, the following questions may be asked of each package:

1. Does it do what you want? Will it perform the functions you require and help you to achieve your objective? The Library Technology Centre at the Polytechnic of Central London provides useful lists of functions which should be offered by different types of software.

2. Does it accommodate your maximum field, record and file sizes?

3. Is it easy to use? Many of the simpler packages are easy to learn, but cumbersome in use. Ask existing customers (the supplier should be able to provide you with a list) about their experience, looking especially at:

   Data Entry. How easy is it to input data and to edit errors made on input? Is it possible to copy data from one record to another to reduce repetitive typing? The amount and type of data to be entered and the staff who will input the data should be considered.

   Validation. Are incorrect data such as dates or ISBNs indicated on input?

   Editing. Is it easy to amend existing data? Some line editors, for example, are slow and difficult to use.

   Changing Modes. How easily and quickly is it possible to switch between functions, such as inputting, editing, searching and printing?

Commands. How easy are the commands to remember and to use?

Help. Is online help available, for which functions and how informative is it?

Implementation. How difficult and time consuming is it to set up the system? Many packages which offer sophisticated facilities require considerable effort to make them perform successfully. How much training and support is available, how good is it and how much will it cost?

4. Is the manual helpful? Look for one which is easy to understand and to use. A good index is essential.

5. Does the software operate at a satisfactory speed? Two programs performing the same task will operate at different speeds, as will the same program on different machines. It is as well to see the software operating on the type of hardware you intend to buy with a realistic size of database, to ensure a satisfactory response time. In particular, how long does it take to update the file? Information retrieval systems which offer fast retrieval, often take longer to update.

6. How reliable is the company? You need to know that you will be offered support; what would happen in the event of either the software developer or the supplier ceasing to trade?

7. What do other customers think about the product and the company? If possible, obtain a **full** list of customers from the supplier.

8. Can you afford it? In addition to the cost of the software, there may be extras, such as the manual, implementation, training, support and maintenance.

9. Is it compatible with other software? If links to other software, such as word processing or online search software are required, will the two packages work? Will it work on existing hardware and, if necessary, operate with an existing printer?

A V CATALOG WRITER

Supplier: Follett Software Company
4506 Northwest Highway, Crystal Lake, IL 60014, USA
Tel: (800)435-6170; (815)455-1100
Hardware: Apple II Plus; Apple IIe; TRS 80 model III
Requirements: 48K RAM and 80 column printer
Price: 89.95 US dollars
Notes: School library audio visual catalogue. Providing searching on up to 3 subjects. Up to 1000 items may be held on one disk. Shelf list and subject catalogues may be printed.
Descriptors: Audio visual materials; catalogues; school libraries

A V EQUIPMENT INVENTORY

Supplier: Media Center Factory
PO Box 13536, Greensboro, NC 27405, USA
Hardware: Apple II; Apple II Plus; Apple IIe; Commodore 64; TRS 80 model I; TRS 80 model III; TRS 80 model IV
Price: 30 US dollars
Descriptors: Audio visual control

A V INVENTORY

Supplier: D and H Software
703 County-Aire Ct., Waunakee, Wis 53597, USA
Hardware: Apple II Plus; Apple IIe
Requirements: 132 column printer
Price: 49.95 US dollars
Notes: Compiles statistics on the value of the equipment and total repairs, updates records when equipment is added or discarded and allows amendment of present records
Descriptors: Audio visual control

ACCESS (TM) - Microcomputer network system

Supplier: Information Intelligence, Inc.
PO Box 31098, Phoenix, AZ 85046, USA
Tel: (800) 228-9982 (except Arizona & Alaska); (602) 996-2283
Operating System: DOS 3.3
Hardware: Apple II; Apple II Plus; Apple IIe
Requirements: Two apple 5.25" disk drives: minimum 48K RAM; clock card, Hayes or Hayes-compatible 300 or 1200 baud modem; supports Apple 80-column cards for Apple IIe.
Price: 250 US dollars for first system; 175 US dollars for each additional system.
Notes: ACCESS (automated computer communication electronic service system) can be used as a microcomputer network communications system or as a bulletin-board system (BBS) or both at the same time. In networking the system automatically sends and receives electronic mail, interlibrary loans, forms, orders, etc. to any other ACCESS system at 300 or 1200 baud (depending on modem used by owner). It can also be accessed by any ASCII terminal or microcomputer over ordinary voice-grade telephone lines. The videotex version of this software program is called "VIDACCESS" which is a "read only" system with up to 100 lines of text per message possible (see "VIDACCESS"). The LOAN (Library Automated Online Network) version is now identical to the standard ACCESS system. Three add-on programs (25 US dollars each - all three for 50 US dollars) include System Name, Auto-Delete, and Auxiliary File.
Review: Please note: references which appear in Rorvig, M.E. "Microcomputers and libraries" are inaccurate.
Descriptors: Bulletin boards; communications; interlibrary loans; electronic mail; viewdata: access to remote systems

ACCESSION PLUS

Supplier: Right On Programs
PO Box 977, Huntingdon, NY 11743, USA
Hardware: Apple IIe; Apple II Plus; Commodore pet; Commodore 64; IBM PC; TRS 80
Requirements: Pet, 32K RAM
Price: 40 US dollars
Notes: Lists books and media collections by title, author or subject. Bibliographies may be prepared. The software allows for brief annotations to be added.
Descriptors: Accessions lists; bibliographies

ACQUEST

Supplier: Central Information Service
Senate House, University of London, Malet Street, London, WC1 7HU, UK
Tel: 01 636 8000 x5089
Operating System: MS DOS; PC DOS
Price: 750 pounds sterling
Notes: The system is built around a main file consisting of bibliographic records with fields for supplier, order number, dates of order and receipt, source of information, requester, fund, number of copies, price, currency and comments. One record relates to one or more copies of an item identified by the ISBN or ISSN. "Status" codes are assigned to indicate which stage the item has reached in the acquisitions process. The system can generate reports in tabular, bibliographic and card formats.
Descriptors: Acquisitions

ACSESS

Supplier: International Coffee Organisation
22 Berners Street, London, W1P 4DD, UK
Tel: 01 580 8591; tlx: 267659
Operating System: DRX 2; DRX 3
Hardware: ICL DRS 20
Requirements: Communications ports
Price: 99 pounds sterling
Notes: External databases may be accessed through dial up and single key entry to up to 10 different hosts. The software can be tailored to speeds of either 300 or 1200 baud. Search results may be displayed on the screen and directed to a disk file for subsequent offline editing and printing using ICL's DTM (Distributed Text Manager) word processing software.
Descriptors: Online search aid

ACTA CRYSTALLOGRAPHICA INDEX SYSTEM

Supplier: Acta crystallographica
International Union of Crystallography, 5 Abbey Square, Chester, CH1 2HU, UK, fao M.H. Dacombe
Tel: 0244 42878
Operating System: OASIS
Price: On application
Notes: Package developed for Acta Crystallographica, but could be used for other applications by arrangement
Descriptors: Book indexes; indexes

ADLIB2

Supplier: Databasix
Strawberry Hill House, Old Bath Road, Newbury, Berkshire, RG13 1NG, UK
Tel: 0635 37373; tlx: 847112 dbasixg
Operating System: UNIX
Requirements: Informix database system
Price: On application (ADLIB2 entry level system 12,480 pounds sterling including hardware, software, documentation and training)
Notes: The catalogue is the foundation of the system. Data is entered on formatted screens and authority control is provided. An online public access catalogue is available, and catalogue lists, reports, search listings etc may be generated from the catalogue in user defined formats. Free text catalogue searching and thesaurus management are available. Acquisitions, serials control and circulation control modules are also features of the system. The software is menu driven.
Descriptors: Acquisitions; catalogues: online; issue system; serials control; thesaurus control

AIM2 - Interlending System

Supplier: Leicester Polytechnic Library
PO Box 143, Leicester, LE1 9BH, UK
Tel: 0533 551551
Operating System: MS DOS; PC DOS
Hardware: IBM PC; IBM PC compatibles
Price: To be announced
Notes: A complete interloans administration system based on an earlier version of AIM.
Review: To AIM. Program 19 Jan 1985, p44; Information on AIM2 from AIM Project at Leicester Polytechnic Library
Descriptors: Interlibrary loans

ALC BASIC LIBRARY SERIES

Supplier: Advanced Library Concepts Inc
1188 Bishop Street, Suite 1511, PO Box 4586, Honolulu, Oahu, Hawaii 96813, USA
Tel: 808 544 0939
Operating System: PC DOS
Hardware: IBM PC XT; IBM PC AT
Price: From 10,400 US dollars for hw and sw; from 3,800 to 5,600 US dollars sw only
Notes: The bibliographic database is the basis of the system. Data record content is fixed but screens for record entry, and display can be user defined so that the display of data fields can be controlled. author or title can be used to obtain a call number at which to browse forward or backward through the database. The circulation module keeps track of changes in status due to circulation activity. Features include: the definition of borrower types; setting of loan periods; reservation of borrowed items. Help messages are available and security codes limit users to modules or to functions. Access levels can be assigned to specific parts. Series 1000 is suitable for libraries with as few as 5,000 volumes (expandable to 20,000) whose primary concern is circulation control with some search capability. Series 2000, 3000 and 4000 are aimed at libraries at 20,000 to 500,000 volumes and support acquisitions and serials check-in.
Descriptors: Acquisitions; catalogues: online; issue system; serials control

APPLE CIRC

Supplier: CTL Library Systems
1455 South State Street, Orem, Utah 84057, USA
Hardware: Apple II; Apple III
Requirements: Hard disk
Price: 1500 to 3500 US dollars
Notes: Versions 2 and 3
Descriptors: Issue system

AQUILA

Supplier: Kent Barlow Information Associates
Kingsmead House, 250 Kings Road, Chelsea, London, SW3 5UE, UK
Tel: 01 351 2776; tlx: 268627
Operating System: CP M
Requirements: 5.25" or 8" disks 48K RAM minimum
Price: 395 pounds sterling
Notes: A larger version of EAGLE offering 2200 character records, database merging and subset generation. Can also be interfaced with some commercial databases. Interface modules are extra. See MAGPIE.
Descriptors: Databases: inhouse; information retrieval

ART PRINT INVENTORY

Supplier: Media Center Factory
PO Box 13536, Greensboro, NC 27405, USA
Hardware: Apple II; Apple II Plus; Apple IIe; Commodore 64; TRS 80 model I; TRS 80 model III; TRS 80 model IV
Price: 20 US dollars
Descriptors: Audio visual control

ARTTEL

Supplier: Leicester Polytechnic Library
City Campus, PO Box 143, Leicester, LE1 9BH, UK
Tel: 0533 551551
Hardware: Commodore pet; Texas Instruments TX700
Requirements: Pet: disk drive, printer and BT type 13a modem; TI: tape deck
Notes: Developed by Taylor Wilson Systems Ltd of Dorridge in conjunction with Leicester Polytechnic Library. Transmits loan request online to BLLD.
Review: Yeadon, J. Size no barrier to ARTTEL loan service. Library Association Record 86 (10) October 1984 p391
Descriptors: Interlibrary loans

ASCOM IV

Supplier: Dynamic Microprocessor Associates
545 Fifth Avenue, New York, NY 10017, USA
Tel: 212 687 7115
Operating System: PC DOS 2.0; MS DOS 2.0
Hardware: IBM PC; IBM PC XT; IBM PC AT; IBM PC compatibles
Requirements: 256K RAM minimum and a standard serial port
Price: 195 US dollars
Notes: Menu driven communications software which permits the user to connect and logon to commonly used databases and time sharing services. There is an online help facility. Terminals emulated include DEC VT100, DEC VT52, ADDS Viewpoint, Televideo 912, IBM 3101, LSI ADM3A, Hazeltine 1500. There are more than 60 commands and a built in editor.
Descriptors: Communications; online search aid

ASSASSIN PC

Supplier: MGS Computing Services
Shoppenhangers Road, Maidenhead, Berks, SL6 2PX, UK
Tel: 0628 39211
Operating System: PC DOS release 2
Hardware: IBM PC XT; IBM PC AT; IBM PC; IBM PC compatibles
Requirements: Tallgrass winchester disk, 256K RAM
Price: 995 pounds sterling
Notes: Microcomputerised version of ASSASSIN. The software permits the storage and retrieval of free form text. Data entry features include prompted direct screen input, and a word processing interface. Items may be allocated to one of nine files and can be classified as confidential for security purposes. Personal names, words and phrases may be indexed. Full text and marked word indexing are possible within a single item. Search facilities include automatic synonym searches, nested Boolean logic, and search limitation by files or dates. There is a string search feature for words not indexed, and full or part display of selected items. Print facilities are available, and output may be to disk for incorporation into other documents. The system features online index maintenance including synonyms. The system has both "novice" and "expert" modes, and a "help" facility.
Review: Assassin PC, Library Micromation News, No11, January 1986, pp 1-3
Descriptors: Information retrieval; databases: inhouse; word processing

ASSIST

Supplier: Userlink Communications Ltd
9, Brabyns Brow, Marple, Stockport, Cheshire, SK6 7DA, UK
Tel: 061 427 7432
Operating System: CP M; CP M-86; MS DOS; PC DOS
Hardware: Apricot; Cifer, Columbia; Compaq; DEC rainbow; IBM PC; IBM PC compatibles; Sirius; Superbrain
Requirements: 64K RAM for 8 bit machines; 128K for 16 bit machines. All require an RS232 (V24) serial communications port
Price: 195 pounds sterling
Notes: ASSIST offers the following features: autologon and protocol storage to enable one key logon to remote computer system; text storage of more than 650 words and phrases and offline editing of text; full speed transmission of stored messages line-by-line or by randomly selected line; downloading and storage of text to disk which may be printed as received or after disconnection; function keys for frequently used commands. The system operates on full or half duplex with xon, xoff flow control of incoming information. Communication and parity speeds are controlled by the user. Text Prestel is available on most versions.
Descriptors: Electronic mail; online search aid; viewdata: access to remote systems

ASSOCIATIVE FILE PROCESSOR

Supplier: Datafusion Corp
5115 Douglas Fir Road, Calabasas, CA 91302, USA
Hardware: DEC micro PDP 11 23
Requirements: Also runs on DEC minis
Price: 42,000 US dollars approximately, including hardware and installation
Notes: Information retrieval package which permits natural language queries and enables statistical analysis on extracted fields. A data load program is provided for data entry which allows the entry of data without field delimiters or demarcations. Retrieved records may be saved and accessed later for report generation. An automatic thesaurus facility is available. SDI profiles can be stored.
Descriptors: Information retrieval; statistics; thesaurus control

ASTRA FINANCIAL JOURNAL

Supplier: NEC Information Systems
Lexington, Maryland, USA
Notes: Interface to Dow Jones News Retrieval database via Telenet or Tymnet
Descriptors: Online access to Dow Jones News Retrieval

AV CARD DIRECTORY PROGRAM

Supplier: Library Processes System
919 W Canadian street, Vinita, OK 74301, USA
Tel: 918 256 8598
Hardware: TRS 80 model III; TRS 80 Model IV; TRS 80 model IVP; TRS 80 model IVD
Requirements: 48K RAM, disk drives, tractor feed printer for cards, 80 column printer for the directory
Price: 225 US dollars
Notes: Permits the creation of an AV software directory as well as sets of cards for the catalogue and shelf list, with a single entry for each item. One card or a full set may be printed including title card, author, shelf list, series and two subject cards. Three lines of description are allowed.
Descriptors: Catalogues: audio visual material

BASIL

Supplier: Cristad
Zac de Mercieres, 60200 - Compiegne, France
Notes: The BASIL software comprises 5 main programs accessed through a menu using natural language dialogue. The system offers an online help program, a connection procedures recording program, an intelligent text editor with line by line syntax analysis enabling the construction of search strategies. A further program is available for executing and modifying the strategy, recording the online session, and connection charge accounting. A fifth program enables the reformatting, sorting, paging and printing of search results.
Descriptors: Online access to CAS online; online access to DARC; online access to Data Star; online access to Dialog; online access to DIMDI; online access to GCAM; online access to Medline; online access to Questel 1; online access to Questel 2; online access to SDC; online search aid

BBC MICRO LIBRARY SYSTEM

Supplier: G & G Software Ltd
The Old Cider House, Fowey, Cornwall, PL23 1LN, UK
Tel: 072683 2315
Hardware: BBC MODEL B
Requirements: 400k disk drive
Price: Housekeeping module 150 pounds sterling; cataloguing module 150 pounds sterling; both modules combined 200 pounds sterling.
Notes: The "housekeeping" system has capacity for up to 2300 borrowers each of which can be limited to a preset number of books up to a maximum of nine. Loan periods can be a standard three weeks or can be set for each book issued. Up to 20,000 books may be held by the system. Books are identified by an accession number and a 20 character short title. However, should the title not be required, the number of books held can be increased to 60,000. Books may be reserved, and warnings are given when reserved books are returned. Overdue notices are produced, and various reports may also be generated. A separate catalogue module is available and allows books to be catalogued and retrieved on words in title, author and Dewey classification number. The capacity of the system is 10,000 books with approximately 60 characters per book.
Descriptors: Catalogues; issue system

BIB BASE

Supplier: Small Library Computing
48 Lawrence Ave, Holbrook, NY 11741, USA
Tel: 516 588 1387
Operating System: MS DOS 1.1+; PC DOS 1.1+; Z DOS 1.1+; CP M-86; MP M-86
Hardware: IBM PC; Zenith Z100
Requirements: Will run on other microcomputers with operating systems listed.
Notes: Not intended as a full online catalogue, but allows creation and maintenance of an indexed database of MARC-tagged bibliographic records. Links with BIB BASE ACQ.
Descriptors: Catalogues

BIB BASE ACQ

Supplier: Small Library Computing
48 Lawrence Ave, Holbrook, NY 11741, USA
Tel: 516 588 1387
Operating System: MS DOS 1.1+; PC DOS 1.1+; Z DOS 1.1+; CP M-86; MP M-86
Hardware: IBM PC; IBM PC XT; Zenith Z100; Zenith Z110; Zenith Z120
Requirements: 192K RAM, dual disk drives and a printer
Notes: Online acquisitions program which can handle up to approximately 64,000 records at the under consideration, on order, in process and recently catalogued stages. See also BIB BASE TEXT.
Descriptors: Acquisitions

BIB BASE ACQ AND BIB BASE CAT COMBINED

Supplier: Small Library Computing
48 Lawrence Ave, Holbrook, NY 11741, USA
Tel: 516 588 1387
Operating System: PC DOS; MS DOS
Hardware: IBM PC; IBM PC XT; IBM PC AT; Zenith Z110; Zenith Z120
Requirements: 192K RAM 2 disk drives and a printer. A hard disk is preferred.
Price: 1345 US dollars
Notes: BIB BASE with the ACQ and the CAT subsystems merged into one program. A function key allows the user to switch between the 2 subsystems. A demonstration version is available for 70 dollars.
Descriptors: Acquisitions; catalogue cards

BIB BASE CAT

Supplier: Small Library Computing
48 Lawrence Ave, Holbrook, NY 11741, USA
Tel: 516 588 1387
Operating System: MS DOS; PC DOS
Hardware: IBM PC; IBM PC XT; IBM PC AT; Zenith Z110; Zenith Z120
Requirements: 192K RAM, 2 disk drives and a printer. A hard disk is preferred.
Price: 895 US dolLars
Notes: An online bibliographical database system for catalogue card production and the printing of cards, pocket and spine labels. Several formats are available, and formatted cards may be formatted on the screen if desired. See also BIB BASE TEXT
Descriptors: Catalogue cards

BIB BASE MARC

Supplier: Small Library Computing
48 Lawrence Ave, Holbrook, NY 11741, USA
Tel: 516 588 1387
Operating System: PC DOS 2.0+
Hardware: IBM PC; IBM PC XT; IBM PC AT; IBM PC compatibles
Requirements: 192K RAM and 2 disk drives
Price: 250 US dollars

Notes: A module which can be added to BIB BASE ACQ or BIB BASE CAT. It allows the loading of full MARC records into the BIB BASE datafile as well as the output of a full MARC record generated from a record in BIB BASE. Auxiliary programs useful in validating and manipulating files of MARC are also included.
Descriptors: Catalogues; data entry; MARC record interface

BIB BASE TEXT
Supplier: Small Library Computing
48 Lawrence Ave, Holbrook, NY 11741, USA
Tel: 516 588 1387
Operating System: PC DOS 2.0+
Hardware: IBM PC; IBM PC XT; IBM PC AT
Requirements: 192K RAM, 2 disk drives
Price: 250 US dollars
Notes: A module which can be added to BIB BASE ACQ or BIB BASE CAT. Records can be input to the BIB BASE datafile from a non BIB BASE source, and BIB BASE records can be output to a disk file for manipulation by other programs.
Descriptors: Data input

BIBLIO BUY
Supplier: Biblio Tech Ltd
124a Dunstable Road, Luton, Beds, LU1 1EW, UK
Tel: 0582 24557
Hardware: Comart
Price: From around 5500 pounds sterling including hardware
Notes: An acquisitions system featuring full fund accounting, order production, receipt and accessioning facilities. Barcode labels may be printed for the items at the ordering or receipt stage. Links to the other "Biblio" systems mean that data may be transferred to the short author/title catalogue without rekeying. Outstanding items are chased automatically and reports of expenditure by fund and subject are possible. BIBLIO BUY may be purchased as a stand-alone module or a starter system which can be extended to other applications. It is menu driven and has a mainframe communications option.
Review: Biblio Tech Systems for college size libraries, VINE 57 December 1984 pp13-
Descriptors: Acquisitions; communications

BIBLIO GUIDE
Supplier: Biblio Tech Ltd
124a Dunstable Road, Luton, Beds, LU1 1EW, UK
Tel: 0582 24557
Hardware: Comart
Price: No details available
Notes: An interactive guiding system for libraries. Information is presented using text and graphics on VDU screens. A librarian can build his/her own. interactive guide.
Descriptors: Library guiding; user education

BIBLIO LEND
Supplier: Biblio Tech Ltd
124a Dunstable Road, Luton, Beds, LUI IEW, UK
Tel: 0582 24557
Hardware: Comart
Notes: Features loan control via 8 reader types and 8 book types. Permits a full bibliographic description of items on loan and full reader details. Up to 64 independent loan periods are supported. Overdue and recall notices may be printed, and there is a reservation module. Management statistics are generated, and barcode data entry is permitted. The software is designed to integrate with other Biblio Tech library housekeeping packages.
Review: Biblio Tech systems for college size libraries VINE 57 December 1984 pp13-
Descriptors: Issue system

BIBLIO LINK
Supplier: Personal Bibliographic Software Inc
PO Box 4250, Ann Arbor, Michigan 48106, USA
Tel: (313) 996-1580
Operating System: CP M; PC DOS; MS DOS
Hardware: Apple Macintosh; IBM PC; IBM PC AT; IBM PC XT; IBM PC compatibles
Requirements: Serial port and modem; 128K RAM, disk drive (double sided for Mac); IBM compatibles must be 100
Price: 195 US dollars
Notes: BIBLIO LINK is a set of companion programs to PRO-CITE and the PROFESSIONAL BIBLIOGRAPHIC SYSTEM. Each program converts records downloaded from an online database into a format acceptable to the two database programs. The various bibliographic elements, such as author, title, and publication date, are transferred into the appropriate fields according to document type. The downloaded records can then be merged with existing, manually entered records or stored in a separate PRO-CITE or PBS database. A separate BIBLIO-LINK is available for each online database. currently available links include: Dialog, BRS, OCLC, and RLIN for IBM computers and Dialog, BRS, and Medlars for the Macintosh. Links for additional online services will be available in the future.
Descriptors: Online access to BRS; Online access to Dialog; online access to Medlars; online access to OCLC; online access to RLIN; reformatting

BIBLIO TEL
Supplier: Biblio Tech Ltd
124a Dunstable Road, Luton, Beds, LU1 1EW, UK
Tel: 0582 24557
Hardware: Comart
Notes: BIBLIO TEL is designed to support and enhance the Telepen level 3 circulation control system. BIBLIO TEL provides a short author/title catalogue and reader file directly linked to the Telepen so that enquiries may be made by a single barcode scan. Overdues and reserve lists may be produced. Data entry, barcode production, catalogue searching and back up and recovery features are included in the package.

Review: Biblio Tech systems for college size libraries VINE 57 December 1984 pp13-
Descriptors: Data entry; issue system

BIBLIOGRAPHY COMPILER
Supplier: Libraries and Learning Inc
210 5th Avenue, New York, NY 10010, USA
Hardware: Apple; Commodore pet; TRS 80
Requirements: TRS 80, cassette
Price: 20 US dollars
Notes: Produces printed bibliographies which can be put on masters for duplication
Descriptors: Bibliographies

BIBLIOGRAPHY WRITER
Supplier: Follett Software Company
4506 Northwest Highway, Crystal Lake, IL 60014, USA
Tel: (800)435-6170; (815)455-1100
Operating System: DOS 3.3
Hardware: Apple II Plus; TRS 80 model III
Requirements: 48K RAM and 80 column printer
Price: Approx 69.95 US dollars
Notes: Allows for the creation of bibliographies which can be printed by author surname, title or call number. The author field has 20 characters for the last name and 10 for the first name. 78 characters are allocated to the title field and 12 characters to the call number field. Users may also add a city, publisher and copyright fields for periodicals. There are fields for source of publication and page numbers.
Review: Anderson, E.S. Bibliography Writer. Access 3 (1) Spring 1983 p14
Descriptors: Bibliographies

BIO SUPERFILE
Supplier: Thompson Henry Ltd
London Road, Sunningdale, Berks SL5 OEP, UK
Tel: 0990 24615 or 22639
Operating System: CP M; MS DOS
Requirements: Z80 or 8088 processor with 64K RAM and dual disk drive
Price: 100 US dollars
Notes: Integrates with BITS to search and print subsets of the BIOSIS database. References may be added from any BITS shipment or from other sources to the library's own database. The BITS references may be searched and results saved for later use. The splitting of files into special groupings and the sorting of search results are possible. The software is menu driven and may be used in conjunction with a word processing program.
Review: Integrates with BITS to search and print subsets of the BIOSIS database. References may be added from any BITS shipment or from other sources to the library's own database. The BITS references may be searched and results saved for later use. The splitting of files into special groupings and the sorting of search results are possible. The software is menu driven and may be used in conjunction with a word processing program.
Descriptors: Information retrieval: commercial database subsets

BITS
Supplier: Thompson Henry Ltd
London Road, Sunningdale, Berks, SL5 OEP, UK
Tel: 0990 24615 or 22639
Operating System: CP M; MS DOS
Price: From 100 US dollars p.a.
Notes: A service offered to BIOSIS (Biosciences Information Service Database) users that matches personal profiles against file updates each month and sends the results on floppy disks. Can be used with BITTERN, BIO SUPERFILE or SCIMATE to search, update, edit and print a personal database of records.
Descriptors: Biosciences information services data; information retrieval: commercial database subsets

BITS: BOEING INTELLIGENT TERMINAL SYSTEM
Supplier: Boeing Computer Services Europe Ltd
19 Fitzroy Street, London, UK
Tel: 01-380-1500
Operating System: PC DOS
Hardware: IBM PC
Price: Modules priced and available separately
Notes: Intelligent terminal software, consisting of several integrated packages providing data entry, text processing, word processing, relational database management, business graphics, spreadsheet and programming. The master package is known as the Intelligent Terminal Workstation, and contains a full screen editor, utilities (including file and disk maintenance) and a communications package which provides teletype compatibility for online communications with remote computers.
Descriptors: Administration; communications; data entry; databases: inhouse; graphics; word processing

BITTERN
Supplier: Kent Barlow Information Associates
Kingsmead House, 250 Kings Road, Chelsea, London, SW3 5UE, UK
Tel: 01 351 2776; tlx: 268627
Notes: Accepts BIOSIS subsets on disk. See BITS
Descriptors: Information retrieval: commercial database subsets

BNS COMPUTER ASSISTED INDEXING PROGRAM
Supplier: Computer Management Associates (Nathan Roseman)
555 Third Street, Brooklyn, NY 11215, USA
Tel: 212 768 4586
Hardware: Commodore 8032
Requirements: 32K RAM, expandable to 96K, dual floppy drive or 1 floppy and 1 hard disk. Recommended printer: TEC Citon starwriter F-10
Price: 1000 US dollars
Notes: This index generating program is menu driven, prompting the user for the necessary formatting and printing information. Letter by letter or word by word sorting are available, and it is possible to mark words or characters to be ignored by the sorting routine.
Review: Fetters, L.K., A guide to seven indexing programs..., Database, December 1985, pp 31-38

Descriptors: Indexes

BOOKDEX

Supplier: Capital Systems Group Inc
11301 Rockville Pike, Kensington, MD 29895, USA
Tel: (301)881-9400
Operating System: TRS DOS; PC DOS
Hardware: IBM PC; IBM PC XT; TRS 80 model II
Requirements: Printer
Price: 450 US dollars
Notes: Indexes books and reports. Entries are sorted and formatted and subject headings are produced. Authority control is available. Data entry is prompted, and entries can be reviewed and edited on the screen.
Descriptors: Book indexes; indexes

BOOKENDS

Supplier: Sensible Software Inc
210 S. Woodward, Suite 229, Birmingham, MI 48011, USA
Tel: (313) 258-5566
Notes: See other entry

BOOKENDS

Supplier: Herbert Blumstein
Softsel House, Central Way, North Feltham Trading Estate, Feltham, Middlesex, TW14 OXQ, UK
Operating System: DOS 3.3
Hardware: Apple II Plus; Apple IIe; Apple III; IBM PC
Requirements: Apple micros minimum 48K RAM and disk drive
Price: 129.95 US dollars
Notes: Reference management system. Allows searching by author, keywords or title. Holds approximately 900 entries. See also "BOOKENDS TRANSLATORS"
Review: Tommervick, M. "Bookends: the Reference Management System". Softalk (August 1983) pp164,166; Smith, Richard L. "Bookends: the Reference Management System: a software review" The Journal of Computers in Mathematics and Science Teaching. (Summer 1983) pp36-37; "Bookends" Cider (January 1984) pp168-9; Taylor, S.I. "Bookends the reference management system". The New England Journal of Medicine, Jan 12th 1984, p 134
Descriptors: Bibliographies; Reference Management

BOOKENDS EXTENDED

Supplier: Sensible Software inc.
210 S. Woodward, Suite 229, Birmingham, Michigan 48011, USA
Tel: (313) 258-5566
Operating System: PRO DOS
Hardware: Apple IIc; Apple IIe
Requirements: 128K RAM, 80 column screen display compatible with hard disk drives and the new 3.5" Unidisk
Price: 149.95 US dollars plus postage and handling; 65 US dollars if BOOKENDS or BOOKENDS PRODOS used. 29 US dollars if BOOKENDS or BOOKENDS PRODOS traded in.
Notes: The BOOKENDS EXTENDED software has the same features as the PRO DOS version with a number of additions. More references may be stored by the system which can be loaded on a hard disk drive. Alphabetical lists of authors and keywords contained in any number of reference files may be produced. It is possible to scroll forward and backward through the selected references on the screen, and up to six formats may be used at the same time.
Descriptors: Bibliographics; reference management

BOOKENDS PRO DOS

Supplier: Sensible Software Inc.
210 S. Woodward, Suite 229, Birmingham, Michigan 48011, USA
Tel: (313) 258-5566
Operating System: PRO DOS
Hardware: Apple II Plus; Apple IIe; Apple IIc
Requirements: 64K RAM, one 5.25" floppy disk drive and a 40 column display monitor
Price: 129.95 US dollars
Notes: A reference management system which allows details of author, title, journal, volume, page number, date, publisher, editors, location and keywords to be stored. Abstracts of up to 760 characters are supported. The software has a word processor quality editor and may be used to prepare bibliographies or alphabetized listings of keywords and authors in the database.
Descriptors: Bibliographies; reference management

BOOKENDS TRANSLATORS

Supplier: Sensible Software Inc
210 S. Woodwards, Suite 229, Birmingham, Michigan 48011, USA
Notes: See other entry

BOOKENDS TRANSLATORS

Supplier: Herbert Blumstein
Softsel House, Central Way, North Feltham Trading Estate, Feltham, Middlesex, TW14 OQX, UK
Operating System: DOS 3.3
Hardware: Apple II Plus; Apple IIe; Apple III
Requirements: 48K RAM
Notes: Needs BOOKENDS. Aids transfer of references from Dialog and Medline to BOOKENDS files
Descriptors: Online access to Dialog; online access to Medline; reformatting

BOOKSHELF

Supplier: Specialist Computer Systems and Software Ltd
Fourth Floor, Goodson Building, Goodson Street, Hanley, Stoke on Trent, Staffordshire, ST1 2AT, UK
Tel: 0782 279110
Notes: See other entry

BOOKSHELF

Supplier: Logical Choice Computer Services Ltd
3 Newtec Place, Magdalen Road, Oxford
OX4 1RE, UK
Tel: 0865 727946

Operating System: PICK

Hardware: Altos; Crystal; GA

Requirements: Minimum 128K RAM

Notes: An integrated modular system offering cataloguing, acquisitions, circulation and serials control. The catalogue and enquiry module is the basis of the system. The bibliographic record can be any length and fields are variable length. The enquiry facility permits word and phrase searching on one or several fields, Boolean searching and right hand truncation. All or parts of the catalogue may be output on paper, disk or microfiche. The acquisitions module works in conjunction with the catalogue so that input of data through acquisitions automatically updates the catalogue for both new items and extra copies of items already in stock. Budgetary control is on a multi-currency basis on both committed and actual expenditure to any number of charge codes. Order numbers are machine generated but can be overridden. Acquisitions also caters for claiming, part or excess receipt, imperfect or damaged items and cancellations. The circulation module controls issues, returns, renewals, reservations, fines and overdues. Management reports may be generated from information held on the system. Serials control and online search modules are also available.

Descriptors: Acquisitions; catalogues; catalogues: online; information retrieval; issue system; online search aid; serials control

BOOKTRAK

Supplier: Richmond Software Corporation
PO Box 5587, San Mateo, CA 94402, USA
Tel: 800 222 6063

Hardware: Apple II Plus; Apple IIe

Requirements: II Plus, 48K RAM; IIe, 64K RAM

Price: 1400 US dollars for the five programs including barwand. Individual programs range from 150 US dollars to 650 US dollars

Notes: The BOOKTRAK library management system is a package of five interacting programs. the circulation system allows the issue and discharge of items using the barwand light pen and barcode labels. The ordering system prints out orders by supplier and totals the figures. When books are received, account balances are updated and the bibliographic data may be transferred to the cataloguing system where Dewey numbers and subject headings can be assigned. A complete set of catalogue cards may then be produced by the card and label printing program. The serials control program permits the storage of title, supplier, frequency, holdings, missing issues and subscription details. Lists of titles, holdings, missing issues and overdue issues may be generated on screen or paper. Data recorded with the floppy disk circulation system can be uploaded to the hard disk system BOOKTRAK I.

Descriptors: Acquisitions; catalogue cards; issue system; serials control

BOOKTRAK I

Supplier: Richmond Software Corporation
PO Box 5587, San Mateo, CA 94402, USA
Tel: 800 222 6063

Operating System: PRO DOS

Hardware: Apple IIe

Requirements: 80 column extended text card and monitor, one floppy disk drive and PRO DOS compatible hard disk, barwand, PRO DOS compatible clock card and program compatible printer with graphics capability

Price: 850 US dollars

Notes: BOOKTRAK I is a hard disk circulation system designed for libraries with collections of 3,000 to 250,000 items. it permits the check-in and out of items using a barcode label scanner, the management of reservations and overdues, and the generation of statistical reports on circulation and analysis of use. The program is menu driven and has help screens which can be called up and dismissed without affecting the previous display or disturbing work in progress. Users of the Booktrak floppy disk circulation system may trade in that program for the hard disk program for 425 US dollars. Data can be uploaded to the hard disk program without retyping.

Descriptors: Issue system

BOOKWORM

Supplier: Hammett Microcomputer Division
Hammett Place, Box 545, Braintree,
Maryland 02184, USA

Hardware: Apple II; Commodore Pet; TRS 80

Price: 59 US dollars

Notes: School library issue system

Descriptors: Issue system; school libraries

BORROWERS FILE

Supplier: Mr Craig
209 Nelson Court East, Madison, TN 37115,
USA

Hardware: TRS 80 Model II

Price: On application

Descriptors: Borrower registration

BRS SEARCH

Supplier: BRS Software Products
1200 Route 7, Latham, NY 12110, USA
Tel: 518 783 1161

Notes: See other entry

BRS SEARCH

Supplier: BRS Europe
11 Weymouth Street, London, W1N 3FG, UK
Tel: 01 580 5271; tlx: 291216 comstu g

Operating System: UNIX; XENIX

Requirements: 512K RAM for single user, plus 256K for each additional user

Price: From 2,450 pounds sterling

Notes: An information retrieval system into which text may be keyed, using the optional word procesing package or loaded in machine readable form. A "file layout" may be created for each database on a "database design form", enabling data to be formatted according to user requirements. BRS SEARCH permits a

maximum of 16 million documents per database, 65,000 paragraphs per document, 225 sentences per paragraph and 255 words per sentence. Online updating is possible. Databases are searched in natural language, and Boolean, positional and nested searching are possible. There is also a root command to display terms beginning with a specific word stem. The system offers right hand, left hand and embedded truncation, and range searching on numbers. There is a SAVE SEARCH facility to enable a user to store a search strategy and execute it at a later time, and user programmable function keys. BRS Searchmate has been developed as a menu driven interface and BRS Maint provides menu driven control of database creation, maintenance and other system wide features.
Descriptors: Databases: inhouse; information retrieval

CALICO
Supplier: Computer Assisted Library Instruction Co Inc
PO Box 15916, St Louis, MO 63114, USA
Tel: (314)394-4500
Operating System: DOS 3.3
Hardware: Apple II Plus; Apple II
Requirements: 48K RAM and disk drive
Price: 29.95 US dollars per module
Notes: Training modules available for: Almanacs, Bartlett's familiar Quotations, Current Biography, Periodical Indexes, Poetry Indexes, and the Library Catalogue
Descriptors: User education

CALL NUMBER ORDER
Supplier: Computer Assisted Library Instruction Co Inc
PO Box 15916, St Louis, MO 63114, USA
Tel: (314)394-4500
Hardware: Apple II
Price: 26.45 US dollars for disk, documentation, p&p
Notes: For teaching the use of Dewey in school libraries. The program can be used for review or testing. A summary of the student's responses is shown at the end of the program.
Descriptors: User education

CALM 3.1: CARD AND LABEL MANAGER
Supplier: Speak Softly Inc
303 Calvert Avenue, Clinton, SC 29325, USA
Tel: 803 833 5407
Operating System: DOS 1.1+; PC DOS
Hardware: Apple II Plus; Apple IIe; Apple IIc; IBM PC; IBM PC compatibles
Requirements: Apple II plus 48K RAM and 2 disk drives; Apple IIe or IIc and IBM PC, 1 or 2 disk drives
Price: Apple II Plus 169 US dollars; Apple IIe, Apple IIc 199 US dollars; IBM PC 249 US dollars
Notes: Production of catalogue cards, card and pocket labels and spine labels. An enhanced version inlcudes a choice of 3 print sizes (10 characters per inch, 16.8 characters per inch, and 12 characters per inch) for most dot matrix printers; full support of letter quality printers, and an option to have contents notes automtically removed from the shelf list card. Owners of earlier versions of CALM can receive the new version for 10.00 US dollars by returning one copy of their program disk to the company.
Descriptors: Catalogue cards; labels

CALM: COMPUTER AIDED LIBRARY MANAGEMENT
Supplier: Pyramid Computer Systems Ltd
9 Church Street, Reading, Berkshire, RG1 2SB, UK
Tel: 0734 595633; tlx: 848278 gilco g
Operating System: PC DOS; PC NET
Hardware: IBM PC XT; IBM PC AT; IBM PC compatibles; Televideo PM16
Requirements: Minimum 10 Mb disk
Price: From 1750 pounds sterling
Notes: Supports cataloguing, circulation, acquisitions and serials control. The system allows a maximum of 100,000 items with 18 keywords of 40 characters per item, and supports a maximum of 100,000 readers. CALM systems are able to communicate with other CALM systems or larger computer services such as BLCMP and BLAISE LOCAS. Remote logon facilities are also possible. See also LIBRARY MANAGEMENT SYSTEM.
Review: microcomputer housekeeping systems: CALM, VINE, May 1986
Descriptors: Acquisitions; catalogues; issue system; serials control; thesaurus control

CARD
Supplier: Capital Systems Group Inc
11301 Rockville PIke, Kensington, MD 20895, USA
Tel: (301)881-9400
Operating System: CP M
Hardware: TRS 80
Price: 300 US dollars
Notes: Prints catalogue cards according to AACR2
Descriptors: Catalogue cards

CARD CATALOG
Supplier: Mr Craig
209 Nelson Court East, Madison, TN 37115, USA
Hardware: TRS 80 model II
Price: On application
Notes: In Microsoft Basic
Descriptors: Accessions lists; catalogue cards; labels

CARD DATALOG
Supplier: DTI Data Trek Inc
621 Second Street, Second Floor, Encinitas, CA 92924, USA
Operating System: CP M; MP M; MS DOS
Price: 5795 US dollars starting price for complete systems including a microcomputer with 10 Mb hard disk, printer, word processing software and one CARD DATALOG module
Notes: Based on dBase II. System features 5 integrated modules: acquisitions, catalogue, circulation, serials and laboratory notebooks
Descriptors: Acquisitions; catalogues; issue system; serials control

CARDPREP

Supplier: Follett Software Company
4506 Northwest Highway, Crystal Lake, IL 60014, USA
Tel: (800)435-6170;(815)455-1100
Hardware: Apple IIe; Apple II Plus; TRS 80 model III; TRS 80 model IV
Requirements: 48K RAM, single disk drive and 80 column printer
Price: 199.95 US dollars
Notes: Produces catalogue cards
Descriptors: Catalogue cards

CARDPRO: APPLE

Supplier: Clinton - Essex - Franklin Library System
PO Box 570, Plattsburgh, NY 12901, USA
Tel: (518)563-5190
Operating System: CP M
Hardware: Apple II Plus; Apple IIe
Requirements: 64K RAM and 80 column board and Microsoft softcard; the printer must be able to handle cards
Price: 50 US dollars
Notes: This program is a typing utility only. The typist enters the main entry of the catalogue card set and the computer prints a complete set of headed cards. Multiple sets can be made from one typing. Up to seven added entries may be entered. Saves approximately two thirds of the typist's time, depending upon the size of the card sets. It is essential that the purchaser have the Microsoft Softcard for the Apple as the program cannot be accessed by the languages resident in the usual Apple II computers.
Descriptors: Catalogue cards; labels

CARDPRO: TRS

Supplier: Hugh Starke
RFD number 1 River Road, Peru, NY 12972, USA
Tel: (518)643-9032
Operating System: TRS DOS
Hardware: TRS 80 model II; TRS 80 model III; TRS 80 model 12; TRS 80 model 16
Requirements: 48K RAM and disk drive; the printer must be able to handle card stock.
Price: Model III 50 US dollars (if only 1 disk drive, 65 US dollars); Models II, 12 and 16 US dollars (75 US dollars if only 1 disk drive)
Notes: This program is a typing utility only. The typist enters the main entry of the catalogue card set and the computer prints a complete set of headed cards. Multiple sets can be made from one typing. Up to 7 added entries may be entered. Saves approximately two thirds of the typist's time, depending upon the size of the card sets.
Descriptors: Catalogue cards; labels

CATALOG CARD AND LABEL WRITER

Supplier: K 12 Micromedia Publishing
6 Arrow Road, Ramsey, NJ 07446, USA
Tel: (201) 825 8888
Hardware: Apple II; Apple II Plus; TRS 80 model III
Requirements: Disk drive and 80 column printer; Apple II Plus, lower case adaptor
Price: 169 US dollars (199 US dollars with lower case adaptor)
Descriptors: Catalogue cards; labels

CATALOG CARD MAKER III

Supplier: Winnebago Software Co.
121, SO. Marshall Caledonia, MN 55921, USA
Tel: (507)724-5411
Operating System: DOS 3.3
Hardware: Apple IIe; Apple IIc
Requirements: Printer
Price: 179.95 US dollars
Notes: Catalog card producing program. Allows for printing entire card set or individual cards by entering data once. Also prints spine, book and pocket labels.
Descriptors: Catalogue cards; labels

CATALOG CARD PROGRAM

Supplier: Library Processes System
919 W Canadian Street, Vinita, OK 74301, USA
Tel: 918 256 8598
Hardware: IBM PC; IBM PC compatibles; Tandy 1000; TRS 80 model III; TRS 80 model IV; TRS 80 model IVP; TRS 80 model IVD
Requirements: 48K RAM, 2 disk system and tractor feed printer
Price: 225 US dollars
Notes: Produces catalogue cards and book lists. New entries may be added and lost or discarded books deleted. Items may be sorted alphabetically by author or numerically by call number. The system supports Dewey, LC or local cataloguing numbers, designates categories and permits subject searches. Can interface with SPINE POCKET CARD LABELS PROGRAM.
Descriptors: Bibliographies; catalogue cards

CATALOGIT

Supplier: Right On Programs
PO Box 977, Huntingdon, NY 11743, USA
Hardware: Apple II Plus; Apple IIe; Commodore pet; Commodore 64; IBM PC; TRS 80
Requirements: Pet, 32K RAM
Price: 70 US dollars. (Includes 500 continuous feed cards)
Notes: Makes catalogue cards for books, computer software, records, tapes, films, film strips and more. The program will print author, title and up to 4 subject cards.
Descriptors: Catalogue cards

CATALOGUE CARDS

Supplier: Central Information Service
University of London, Senate House, Malet Street, London, WC1E 7HU, UK
Tel: 01 636 8000 x 5089
Operating System: MS DOS; PC DOS
Hardware: Apricot; IBM PC; IBM PC XT; IBM PC AT; IBM PC compatibles; Sirius
Price: 200 pounds sterling
Notes: The software is designed to operate in conjunction with databases created using either MIRABILIS (information retrieval system) or ACQUEST (acquisitions system). The software prints

catalogue cards in user-defined formats and includes facilities for producing added entries.
Descriptors: Catalogue cards

CHECKMATE

Supplier: Capital Systems Group Inc
11301 Rockville Pike, Kensington, MD 20895, USA
Tel: (301)881-9400
Notes: See other entry

CHECKMATE

Supplier: CLASS
1415 Koll Circle, Suite 101, San Jose, CA 95112-4698, USA
Tel: (408)289-1756
Operating System: PC DOS
Hardware: IBM PC; IBM PC XT
Requirements: Printer
Price: 2500 US dollars. 600 dollars per annum maintenance
Notes: Manages up to 2000 serials records (floppy disk version) or up to 6000 records or more in the hard disk version. Provides check in, claiming, routing, acquisitions, searching and management information facilities. See CHECKMATE MTS.
Descriptors: Serials control

CHECKMATE MTS

Supplier: CLASS
1415 Koll Circle, Suite 101, San Jose, CA 9512-4698, USA
Tel: (408)289-1756
Operating System: XENIX
Hardware: TRS 80 model 16
Requirements: Minimum 8 Mb hard disk
Price: 4500 US dollars
Notes: Multi user version of CHECKMATE for up to 3 users. Currently in use in two institutions
Descriptors: Serials control

CIRC

Supplier: Information Systems Design
23 Arthur Road, Erdington, Birmingham, B24 9EX, UK
Tel: 021 384 1524
Operating System: MS DOS 2.11
Hardware: Apricot; Epson HX-20
Price: Software and hardware for 10,000 readers and 100,000 books: less than 10,000 pounds sterling. Software and hardware for 1,000 readers and 15,000 books less than 5,500 pounds sterling. The software package starts at 995 pounds sterling.
Notes: CIRC provides all the normal functions expected for circulation control and is suitable for libraries up to large college size. Menus together with on screen and printed documentation guide the user through the various functions. Multiple loan periods and borrower categories are supported, as are a variety of traps and messages for books and borrowers. Issues, returns and other transactions are processed by reading barcodes. Epson HX-20 portable micros are used as the barcode data capture unit, and up to four of these can be supported online. In addition they can be used offline to log transactions during a power cut, and taken to the shelves for stock taking. The software permits the printing of standard letters or barcode labels and the printing of overdue notices to take place concurrently with online circulation. Transaction and stock usage statistics are maintained.
Descriptors: Issue system

CIRCA I

Supplier: Highsmith Co Inc
PO Box 800, Highway 106 East, Fort Atkinson, Wisconsin 53538, USA
Hardware: Apple IIe; Apple III; IBM PC XT
Requirements: Minimum 5Mb disk
Descriptors: Issue system

CIRCA II

Supplier: MSC Computers
1455 South State Street, Orem, Utah 84058, USA
Tel: (801)224 1169
Hardware: Apple III; IBM PC; IBM PC XT
Requirements: 256K RAM minimum; minimum 5 Mb disk; IBM, Profile or Corvus and optional Intermec light pen; IBM PC with hard disk expansion unit.
Price: 2750 US dollars. 275 US dollars annual maintenance. 805 US dollars barcode reader.
Notes: CIRCA II provides circulation and cataloguing systems. All users and items are assigned machine readable barcodes. Overdue notices are printed for any time period specified, and lists of users with overdue books may be generated. The system supports flexible borrower records to suit either the public, school, academic or special library. The online catalogue allows a maximum of 15 fields, each of which can be one to 225 characters in length. More than one entry can be made on the same record for that field, allowing for multiple authors or subjects. Any or all of the fields can be keyworded. The system contains a bibliographic reporting facility and can produce shelf lists or a complete card catalogue. Collects statistics and produces reports at any time for any length of reporting period. Supports 50,000 records and 8,000 borrowers.
Descriptors: Catalogues; catalogues: online; issue system

CIRCULATION MANAGEMENT SYSTEM

Supplier: Orchard Systems
207 East Third Street, Waunakee, WI 53597, USA
Tel: (608)849-5727
Operating System: DOS 3.3
Hardware: Apple II Plus; Apple IIe
Requirements: 48K RAM, disk drive and 132 column printer
Price: 150 US dollars
Notes: Tracks up to 600 items per disk controlling fine calculations, overdue notice production and providing management information.
Descriptors: Issue system

CIRCULATION MANAGER

Supplier: Microsolutions
1305 West 96 Street, Indianapolis, Indiana 46260, USA
Tel: (317)844-1184
Notes: Controls the circulation of books, serials and audio visual materials. The program caters for overdue materials and prints overdue notices with user defined messages. A variety of customised reports may be generated. The software includes a password system.
Descriptors: Audio visual control; issue system

CIRCULATION PLUS

Supplier: Follet Software Company
4506 Northwest Highway, Crystal Lake, IL 60014, USA
Tel: (800)435-6170; (815)455-1100
Hardware: Apple II Plus; Apple IIe; TRS 80 model III; TRS 80 model IV
Requirements: 48K RAM, hard disk drive, barcode wand and labels and 80 column printer
Price: 695 US dollars
Descriptors: Issue system

HEADLINE

Supplier: Head Computers Ltd
Oxted Mill,Spring Lane,Oxted,Surrey,RH8 9PB,UK
Tel: 08833 7057/5580; tlx: 957525 oxmill g
Operating System: CP M; CP M-86; MS DOS
Hardware: Apricot; Sirius; BBC; CAL PC; Cifer 18xx series; Cifer 28xx series; Columbia PC; Comart; Compaq PC; Cromenco System three; DEC rainbow; HP 150; IBM PC; IBM PC XT; IBM PC AT; Olivetti M21; Olivetti M24; Shelton sig/net; Sperry PC; Superbrain; Torch C500; Victor 9000; Wordplex PC; Zenith PC.
Requirements: Apple II needs CP/M card; BBC needs Z80 card
Price: 120 pounds sterling to 260 pounds sterling for CP/M-80 systems depending on the level of support required. 130 pounds sterling to 280 pounds sterling for MS/PC DOS and CP/M-86 systems. These prices are exclusive of VAT.
Notes: Connects to mainframes and public networks. Integrates with HEADFORM and INMAGIC. HEADLINE allows input to be pre-stored on disk and uploaded when required, permitting search strategies, complex commands and logging on procedures to be set up in advance. Input may be viewed before being sent and adjustments may be made. Data may be transmitted line by line or "en bloc". Output and/or input can be recorded on disk for later display or printing. Integration with a word processing package is possible for subsequent editing and reformatting of search results before printing.
Descriptors: Communications; online search aid; reformatting

COMPUTER CAT: MULTI USER

Supplier: Winnebago Software Co.
121 So. Marshall Caledonia, MN 55921, USA
Tel: (507)724-5411
Operating System: DOS 3.3
Hardware: Apple IIe
Requirements: 1 floppy disk drive, 1 Corvus hard disk, printer and Omninet disk server and Omninet transporter for each station
Price: 995 US dollars
Notes: Computerised card catalogue replacement. Handles 54,000 titles.
Review: Armstrong, M. and Costa, B. Computer Cat at Mountain View Elementary School. Library Hi Tech (Winter 1983) pp47-52
Descriptors: Bibliographies; catalogues; catalogues: online

CONNECT

Supplier: Learned Information (Europe) Ltd
Woodside, Hinksey Hill, Oxford, OX1 5AU, UK
Tel: 0865-730275
Operating System: CP M; MS DOS; PC DOS
Requirements: Runs on 8-bit machines (eg Wren) and 16-bit machines (eg IBM PC compatibles). Please contact supplier for information about availability of program for specific machines.
Price: 125 pounds sterling. Demonstration copy 15 pounds sterling
Notes: An intelligent terminal package, designed for online database access and downloading, Prestel emulation and use of electronic mail services. Macro commands can be stored on user-defined function keys to allow automated logon etc. Can store parameters of 22 remote host computers. Some versions (16-bit only) include EPAD protocol for use with Multistream and automatic log of usage. Back-to-back file transfer possible in all versions.
Descriptors: Communications; online search aid

COPYLINK

Supplier: US Digital Corp
5699D International Way, Milwaukie, OR 97222, USA
Tel: 503 654 0688
Operating System: CP M; PC DOS
Hardware: Apple; IBM PC; IBM PC compatibles
Requirements: CP/M system software on Apple; Hayes and Hayes compatible modems.
Price: 99.95 US dollars
Notes: It is possible to upload and download searches, and store and send sequences. A telephone directory containing up to 10 telephone numbers may be created (although the system will hold more if required) through the use of a text editor. Telephone numbers are not matched with logon strings by the system.
Descriptors: Communications; online search aid

CORMORANT

Supplier: Kent Barlow Information Associates
Kingsmead House, 250 Kings Road, Chelsea, London, SW3 5UE, UK
Tel: 01 351 2776; tlx: 268627
Notes: N.H.S. administrative information systems linking filing system and administrative word processing. The system indexes locations where all related information may be found.
Descriptors: Administration; word processing

CORTEX
Supplier: British Library, Bibliographic Services
2 Sheraton Street, London, W1V 4BH, UK
Tel: 01 636 1544
Operating System: CP M
Hardware: Sirius; Victor 9000
Requirements: Teletype emulation at 300 and 1200 baud
Notes: To help library staff work with British Library automated systems and other online databases, CORTEX provides a local interface for the information retrieval and cataloguing services of the British Library. Records can be entered directly from the keyboard of the microcomputer, received via a telecoms link from the BLAISE LINE files or recalled from a stored file on floppy disk. Records in the correct format can be submitted for LOCAS processing or used locally.
Descriptors: Catalogues; catalogues: online; online access to Blaise-line; online search aid

CREATE
Supplier: Microdex
3000 Pemberley Court, Suite 3, West Lafayette, IN 47906, USA
Operating System: DOS 3.3
Hardware: Apple II Plus; Apple IIe
Requirements: 48K RAM
Price: 80 US dollars plus 2.50 US dollars p and p
Notes: Customized reference statistics program. Statistical reports may be structured. The user is prompted by the program to develop unique programs for statistics collection requirements.
Descriptors: Statistics

CROSSTALK
Supplier: Microstuf Inc
1845 The Exchange, Suite 140, Atlanta, Georgia 30039, USA
Tel: (404) 952-0267
Notes: See other entry

CROSSTALK
Supplier: Tandata Marketing Ltd
Albert Road North, Malvern, Worcester, WR14 2TL, UK
Tel: 06845 68421; tlx: 337617
Operating System: CP/M-86; MS DOS; PC DOS
Hardware: IBM PC; IBM PC compatibles; TI professional; Victor 9000; Wang PC
Requirements: 96K RAM, modem and communications interface
Price: 195 US dollars
Notes: Intelligent terminal software available in a variety of versions. Version 3.6, one of the latest available, offers such features as reverse video highlighting, editing, modifying and autodialling. Current owners of a previous version of CROSSTALK can exchange it for the updated software that offers access to Lexis, Nexis, and other Mead Data Central services. The replacement fee varies up to $30 depending on the version and purchase date of the original software. Version 3.6 is available from Mead Data Central. (See CROSSTALK XVI)
Descriptors: Communications; online search aid

CROSSTALK XVI
Supplier: Microstuf Inc
1845 The Exchange, Suite 140, Atlanta, Georgia 30039, USA
Tel: (404) 952-0267
Notes: See other entry

CROSSTALK XVI
Supplier: Mead Data Central Ltd
PO Box 1803, Dayton, Ohio 45401, USA
Notes: Intelligent terminal software available in a variety of versions. Version 3.6, one of the latest available, offers such features as reverse video highlighting, editing, modifying and autodialling. Current owners of a previous version of CROSSTALK can exchange it for the updated software that offers access to Lexis, Nexis, and other Mead Data Central services. The replacement fee varies up to $30 depending on the version and purchase date of the original software. Version 3.6 is available from Mead Data Central.
Descriptors: Communications; online search aid

CTI
Supplier: Computer Translation Inc
1455 South Street, Suite 3, Orem, UT 84057, USA
Hardware: Apple
Requirements: 48K RAM
Notes: Supports data entry to CLSI
Descriptors: Catalogues; catalogues: online; CLSI: data entry to; data entry

CURRENT TITLES SYSTEM
Supplier: Central Information Service
University of London, Senate House, Malet Street, London WC1E 7HU, UK
Tel: 01 636 8000 x 5089
Operating System: CP M; MS DOS; PC DOS
Hardware: Apricot; IBM PC; IBM PC AT; IBM PC XT; Sirius; Superbrain
Price: 200 pounds sterling (150 pounds sterling to staff of University of London)
Notes: Current awareness or information bulletin production with KWIC or KWOC title indexes, author/name indexes, and subject indexes. Designed to operate in conjunction with the MIRABILIS software. Enables the generation and printing of bulletins.
Descriptors: Bibliographies

DATA TRANSFER SYSTEM
Supplier: Personal Bibliographic Software Inc.
PO Box 4250, Ann Arbor, MI 48106, USA
Tel: (313)996-1580
Hardware: Apple II; Apple II Plus; Apple IIe; IBM PC; Victor 9000
Requirements: 64K RAM, dual disk drive, serial interface, modem and printer
Price: 200 US dollars
Notes: Downloads and reformats records from online library catalogues such as OCLC and RLIN to form a bibliography. Integrates with PERSONAL BIBLIOGRAPHIC SYSTEM to compile, edit and manage bibliographies.
Descriptors: Bibliographies; downloading; reformatting

DATABASE FINDING AID
Supplier: Alert Consultants DFA
7725 Wilson Avenue, Bryon Center, MI 49315, USA
Hardware: Apple II; Apple IIe; IBM PC
Price: 49.95 US dollars
Notes: Covers 700 databases provided through 15 popular search services. Each of the databases is listed by search service and file number or access code. DIF, ASCII TEXT or DBMASTER readable
Descriptors: Online search aid

DATAFAX
Supplier: All Easy Corporation, Vertical Software Division
PO Box 10459, Marina del Rey, CA 90292, USA
Tel: (213)827 8500
Operating System: PC DOS
Hardware: Apple; IBM PC; IBM PC compatibles
Requirements: IBM minimum 256K RAM, Apple 64K RAM.
Notes: A free form filing system. Information is typed onto a blank screen, and keywords are user defined on input. The software is menu driven, and help screens are available. Each record or "folder" can be filed by up to 100 different keywords. Boolean "and" and "or" logic is available, and truncation and range searching are possible.
Descriptors: Databases: inhouse; information retrieval

DATALINK
Supplier: CLSI Ltd
Regent Arcade House, 252-260 Regent Street, London, W1R 5DA, UK
Tel: 01 437 8090
Price: 2.50 US dollars per search
Notes: See other entry

DATALINK
Supplier: CLSI Inc
1220 Washington Street, West Newton, MA 02165, USA
Tel: 617 965 6310
Hardware: CLSI terminal
Price: 2.50 US dollars per search
Notes: DATALINK allows access from a CLSI terminal to online databases and automation systems. The software provides auto dial and auto logon facilities, monitors usage and maintains accounts. It is suitable for use by end users or intermediaries. Online databases which can be accessed include: ALANET; BRS; Dialog; Easynet and Wilsonline. IAC's search helper is part of the DATALINK configuration and provides the user with simplified searching of online files maintained by Dialog, including Legal Resource Index, Magazine Index, Management Contents, National Newspaper Index, Newsearch and Trade and Industry Index.
Descriptors: Online search aid; online access to ALANET; online access to BRS; online access to CLSI; online access to Dialog; online access to Easynet; online access to Wilsonline

DATAPATH
Supplier: ADP Network Services
175 Jackson Plaza, Ann Arbor, MI 48106, USA
Operating System: PC DOS
Hardware: IBM PC
Price: 235 US dollars including training and documentation
Notes: Data access software package allowing the retrieval of information from remote and local databases. Links ADP's central computer systems which support more than 35 financial investment and economic files. Information required may be accessed, selected and downloaded. Hard copy displays can be created.
Descriptors: Information retrieval; online search aid

DATE DUE
Supplier: William L. Brown
8781 Lee Road, Brighton, MI 48116, USA
Operating System: Commodore DOS
Hardware: Commodore 2001; Commodore 4016; Commodore 4032; Commodore 8032; Commodore 64
Requirements: Disk drive
Price: 29.50 US dollars
Notes: Manages the circulation of materials in a small library. Maximum number of transactions depends on hardware, for example 52 in a 16K PET, 200 in a 32K PET, 265 in a Commodore 64
Review: SCIL (3) 10 October 1983 pp4-5
Descriptors: Issue system

DIALOGLINK
Supplier: Micromedia Ltd.
158 Pearl Street, Toronto, Ontario, Canada, M5H IL3
Tel: (416) 593-5211; Toll free: 1-800-387-2689
Notes: See other entry

DIALOGLINK
Supplier: Dialog Information Services Inc.
3460 Hillview Avenue, Palo Alto, CA 94304, USA
Operating System: DOS 2.0+
Hardware: Compaq; IBM PC; IBM PC XT; IBM PC AT; IBM PC compatibles.
Requirements: Minimum memory 256K
Price: 125 US dollars; 95 US dollars for communications manager only; 45 US dollars account manager only; evaluation disk 10 US dollars
Notes: Allows one step access to Dialog once the user's password, local network telephone number and equipment identification have been entered. Access to Dialog from outside the United States is supported, including instructions for setting local access protocols. Search strategies may be created and edited before going online, and searches may be interrupted, modified and continued whilst online. It is possible to type in a command or series of commands whilst Dialog is processing a search request, and the system will automatically execute the commands in the order they were entered. A companion account manager program is also available for keeping track of online costs for cost

accounting. Reports may be generated. Other online services can be added to your "service directory".
Descriptors: Online access to Dialog; online search aid

DIALTERM
Supplier: Legal Technology Group
59 South Eaton Place, London, SW1W 9JJ, UK
Tel: 01 730 8040
Hardware: BBC
Requirements: Full duplex modem
Price: Less than 200 pounds sterling with modem
Notes: Aids online access to Dialog files. Operates at 1200/75 baud
Descriptors: Online access to Dialog

DRM TELETYPE EMULATOR
Supplier: Howson Algraphy
Coal Road, Leeds, LS14 2AL, UK
Tel: 0532 732442; tlx: 557023
Operating System: MS DOS
Hardware: Sirius
Notes: Enables a Sirius micro to be attached to any mainframe that supports asynchronous teletype protocol. Can be used to retrieve and store information from databases on remote mainframe, after which the stored information may be manipulated at will
Descriptors: Communications; online search aid

DYNIX
Supplier: Biblio Tech Ltd
124A Dunstable Road, Luton, Beds, LUI IEW, UK
Tel: 0582 24557
Notes: See other entry

DYNIX
Supplier: Dynix (UK) Ltd
124A Dunstable Road, Luton, Beds, LUI IEW, UK
Tel: 0582 24557
Operating System: PICK
Requirements: PICK computers supporting from 4 users upwards
Notes: Cataloguing and circulation modules. The cataloguing module allows searching on author, title, keyword in title, subject and Library of Congress card number. Truncated searching is possible. Enhancements for the searching mode include browsing, various display levels, and "see" and "see also" references. The system offers variable field lengths, online editing, and online help screens and prompts. There is a public access module restricted to enquiry mode only. The circulation module generates overdue and fines notices and bills. Borrower traps are available, and statistics and reports may be generated. The query language for the system is based on simple English with system wide variable field and record sizes. There are 6 security levels and unlimited passwords.
Review: The DYNIX Library Automation System VINE 58 March 1985 pp 10-15
Descriptors: Catalogues; catalogues: online; issue system

EAGLE
Supplier: Kent Barlow Information Associates
Kingsmead House, 250 Kings Road, Chelsea, London, SW3 5UE, UK
Tel: 01 351 2776; tlx: 268627
Operating System: CP M 2.2; PC DOS
Hardware: Apple II; DEC rainbow; IBM PC; Rediffusion teleputer; Sirius
Requirements: Any CP/M machine with 48K RAM minimum, dual disks, VDU with cursor control
Price: 155 pounds sterling
Notes: Information retrieval system which uses the common command language for searching. Database may include books, magazines, pamphlets or articles. A smaller version of AQUILA (472 character records)
Descriptors: Catalogues; databases: inhouse; information retrieval

EASTWIND
Supplier: UTLAS Inc.
80 Bloor Street West, 2nd Floor, Toronto, Ontario, Canada, M5S 2VI
Tel: (416)923 0890; tlx:065-24479
Operating System: PC DOS; Apple DOS
Hardware: Apple IIe; Apple IIc; Apple III; Data General micros; IBM PC XT
Price: 2500 US dollars. Volume discounts available
Notes: The EASTWIND circulation system performs circulation functions in both stand alone and network arrangement for special collections or smaller libraries. It can also serve as a backup for ALIS I, ALIS II, and ALIS III circulation systems. The software includes the support of full MARC records, specification of MARC fields to be included in the bibliographic database, and the support of a bibliographic database whose size is limited only by the capacity of the disk storage.
Descriptors: Issue system

ELEMENTARY LIBRARY MEDIA SKILLS
Supplier: Commbase Inc
Suite 890, 333 Sibley Street, St. Paul, MN 55101, USA
Operating System: OS 3.3
Hardware: Apple II Plus; Apple IIe
Price: 125 US dollars per module
Notes: For use in school libraries. Module one: Discovering available resources, Module two: Organisation of resources, Module three: locating resources, Module four; research and study skills.
Descriptors: School libraries; user education

ELEMENTARY OVERDUE COLLECTOR
Supplier: Follett Software Company
4506 Northwest Highway, Crystal Lake, IL 60014, USA
Tel: (800)435-6170;(815)455-1100
Hardware: Apple II Plus; TRS 80 model III
Requirements: 48K RAM and 80 column printer
Price: 49.95 US dollars
Descriptors: Overdue notices

ELEMENTARY OVERDUE WRITER

Supplier: Follett Software Company
4506 Northwest Highway, Crystal Lake, IL 60014, USA
Tel: (800)435-6170;(515)455-1100
Operating System: OS 3.3
Hardware: Apple II Plus; Apple IIe; TRS 80 model II; TRS 80 model IV
Requirements: 48K RAM, single disk and 80 column printer
Price: 149.95 US dollars
Descriptors: Overdue notices

ESATERM

Supplier: Legal Technology Group
58 South Eaton Place, London, SW1W 9JJ, UK
Tel: 01 730 8040
Hardware: BBC
Requirements: Full duplex modem
Price: Less than 200 pounds sterling with modem
Notes: Aids online access to ESA/IRS DIALTECH files. Operates at 1200/75 baud
Descriptors: Online access to ESA IRS Dialtech

F.I.L.L.S: FAST INTERLIBRARY LOANS AND STATISTICS 2.0

Supplier: Macneal Hospital, Finance Department/F.I.L.L.S
3249 S Oak Park Avenue, Berwyn, Illinois 60402, USA
Tel: (312) 795 3089
Operating System: PC DOS
Hardware: IBM PC; IBM PC XT; IBM PC AT; OCLC M300 workstation
Price: 360 US dollars; 430 US dollars with Easy Link communications software
Notes: An enhanced version of the F.I.L.L.S package, F.I.L.L.S. 2.0 permits the printing of mailing labels for those libraries from which items have been borrowed. There is a facility to assign "departmental" codes to each record so that items borrowed for each department within an organisation may be reported upon and costed. Requests may be sent to a batch file for electronic transmission which must be achieved outside the F.I.L.L.S. program.
Review: Brooks, J. F.I.L.L.S. 2.0: improved for interlibrary loans Electronic Library 4 (3) 1986 pp144-145
Descriptors: Electronic mail; interlibrary loans

F.I.L.L.S: FAST INTERLIBRARY LOANS AND STATISTICS

Supplier: MacNeal Memorial Hospital, Finance department/F.I.L.L.S
3249 S. Oak park Avenue, Berwyn, IL 60402, USA
Tel: (312) 795 3089
Operating System: PC DOS
Hardware: IBM PC; IBM PC XT; IBM PC AT; OCLC M300 workstation
Price: 360 US dollars without telecommunication; 495 US dollars with FILLS On Tyme; 100 US dollars On Tyme modules as an add on
Notes: A menu-driven interlibrary loan system for filling interlibrary loan forms for printing or delivery by electronic mail, and keeping related statistics. For transfer by electronic mail, a telecommunications package and modem are required for use with CLASS' On Tyme. FILLS PC version has the capacity for 400 outstanding loans, 400 library address and up to 1,000 periodical titles; the IBM PC XT and AT versions cater for up to 2,000 outstanding loans, 1,600 library addresses and 3,200 periodical titles. FILLS is designed to print on the ALA approved 4 part continuous interlibrary loan forms and conforms to ALA standards when transmitting requests via electronic mail.
Review: Brooks, J.A. F.I.L.L.S., Fast Library loans & Statistics. Electronic Library, 3 (1) 1985, pp28-29; Ben-Shir, R. Fast inter-library loans and statistics: the second, enhanced release, Library Software Review, 4 (3), 1985, pp 132-138
Descriptors: Electronic mail; interlibrary loans

FACTFINDER

Supplier: P&P Micro Distributors Ltd
New Hall Hey Road, Rossendale, Lancashire, BB4 6JG, UK
Tel: 0706-217744
Hardware: Apple Macintosh
Requirements: 128K or 512K RAM
Price: 139 pounds sterling plus VAT
Notes: FACTFINDER is a free-text filing system for the Macintosh and includes a built-in text editor. Entries may be totally unstructured and of variable lengths. FACTFINDER will search for any record which contains a specified keyword, which has been previously highlighted as such. The search statement may contain Boolean operators, ranges and word stems.
Review: Lewis, M., Factfinder: a free-text database, Practical Computing, July 1985, p73.
Descriptors: Information retrieval; databases: inhouse; word processing

FACTFINDER

Supplier: Forethought Inc
Mountain View, California, USA
Notes: See other entry

FICTION FINDER

Supplier: Computer Assisted Library Instruction Co Inc
PO Box 15916, St. Louis, MO 63114, USA
Hardware: Apple II Plus; Apple IIe
Price: 39.95 US dollars plus 1.50 US dollars p and p; 6.95 US dollars for manual
Notes: Enables borrowers to locate titles according to their interests
Descriptors: Catalogues; catalogues: online

FILM BOOKING

Supplier: King County Library
300 Eighth Avenue, North Seattle, WA 98109, USA
Operating System: MP M
Hardware: Altos ACS 8000-10
Requirements: Hard disk
Price: 3000 US dollars

Notes: Film handling system which runs on a multi-user micro. The basic program can be customised or enhanced by an outside consulting firm, which may add between 3000 to 5000 US dollars to the total price.
Review: KCLS Film Reservation System. Access: Microcomputers in Libraries 2 (2) 1982
Descriptors: Audio visual control

FINDER
Supplier: Aaron Smith Associates Inc
Suite 518, 1422 West Peachtree Street, NW, Atlanta, Georgia 30309, USA
Tel: (404) 876-0085
Price: 1495 US dollars
Notes: see other entry.

FINDER
Supplier: Pyramid Computer Systems Ltd
9 Church Street, Reading, Berkshire RG1 25B, UK
Tel: 0628 73322; tlx: 848278 GILCO G
Operating System: MS DOS; PC DOS
Hardware: IBM PC; IBM PC XT; TRS 80 Model II; TRS 80 Model 12; TRS 80 Model 16
Price: 1495 US dollars including 2 hours database and application design support
Notes: Free text retrieval system using inverted file technique. Both right and left hand truncation are possible and other features include: masking characters within words; Boolean searching; flexible display and print options; a choice of stop words; searching of all fields in a record or selective searching of a specific field; and fast browsing
Review: Small Computers in Libraries 4 (5) p4 May 1984
Descriptors: Information retrieval; databases: inhouse

FOCUS
Supplier: Ford & Co (South Shields) Ltd
Tyne Dock, South Shields, Tyne and Wear, NE33 5ST, UK
Tel: 091 4540141; tlx: 537539
Hardware: ICL DRS 20
Price: 300 pounds sterling plus VAT
Notes: Multi access computer system which provides storage, cataloguing and retrieval functions user defined with references.
Descriptors: Catalogues; information retrieval

GOLDEN RETRIEVER
Supplier: CLASS
1415 Koll Circle, Suite 101, San Jose, CA 95112-4698, USA
Tel: 408 289 1756
Notes: See other entry

GOLDEN RETRIEVER
Supplier: Capital Systems Group Inc
11301 Rockville Pike, Kensington, MD 20895, USA
Tel: (301)881 9400
Operating System: PC DOS; MS DOS; TRS DOS
Hardware: IBM PC; IBM PC XT; TRS 80 model II; TRS 80 model 12; TRS 80 model 16
Requirements: Printer
Price: 1800 US dollars
Notes: Allows the creation of databases by responding to a series of commands and prompts. Record formats may be designed to suit local needs, and records may be added, deleted, modified or indexed. Keyword access with Boolean operators is possible and the system allows the sorting of records and the generation of reports. GOLDEN RETRIEVER is menu driven software.
Descriptors: Databases: inhouse; indexes; information retrieval

GOLDTERM
Supplier: Legal Technology Group
58 South Eaton Place, London, SW1W 9JJ, UK
Tel: 01 730 8040
Hardware: BBC
Requirements: Full duplex modem
Price: Less than 200 pounds sterling with modem
Notes: Aids online access to the Telecom Gold Service. Operates at 1200/75 and 1200/1200 bauds.
Descriptors: Online access to Telecom Gold

GPO LASERFILE (TM)
Supplier: Library Systems and Services, Inc. (A Gaylord Company)
1395 Piccard Drive, Suite 100, General Motors Building, Rockville, MD 20850, USA
Tel: (800)638 8725
Hardware: IBM PC; IBM PC compatibles; OCLC M300 workstation
Price: 6,995 US dollars (including hardware, software and documentation); maintenance 325 US dollars p.a.; quarterly updates 1,600 US dollars
Notes: References to US government publications in MARC format on video laser disc. Records accessible by LC Card Number, Superintendent of Documents (SUDOC) Number, and title/author key. Once a record is retrieved, it can be manipulated, fully edited and stored reflecting your charges. GPO LASERFILE is designed to interface with the OCLC M300, IBM PC, and other IBM compatible terminals. It can be used with the M300 system to produce catalogue cards and labels for GPO documents.
Descriptors: Information retrieval: commercial database subsets

HEADFORM
Supplier: Head Computers Ltd
Oxted MIll, Spring Lane, Oxted, Surrey, RH8 9PB, UK
Tel: 08833 7057/5580; tlx: 957525 oxmill g
Operating System: CP M; CP M-86; MS DOS
Price: 130 pounds sterling to 280 pounds sterling for CP/M-80 systems. 190 pounds sterling to 340 pounds sterling for HEADFORM PLUS on MS/PC DOS or CP/M-86. Prices are exclusive of VAT. They vary according to the level of support required.
Notes: Data may be transferred between software with different record formats. Records may be restructured when modifying an existing data management application. It is possible to download records from

online databases and upload data to centralised computer systems using the HEADFORM software. Microcomputer software formats handled include Wordstar Mailmerge, Datastar, Cardbox, INMAGIC, Lotus 1-2-3, DMS Delta. Online formats currently include Blaise, Blackwell Technical Services, Pergamon, Datastar, SDC. Dialog and ESRIN are currently being checked out. Integrates with HEADLINE.

HEADLINE: incorrectly listed, please see p.12.

HEADSET

Supplier: Head Computers Ltd
Oxted Mill, Spring Lane, Oxted, Surrey, RH8 9PB, UK
Tel: 08833 7057/5580; tlx: 957525 oxmill g
Operating System: PC DOS; MS DOS; CP M-86
Hardware: Apricot; HP 150; IBM PC; IBM PC XT; IBM PC AT; DEC rainbow; Sirius; Victor 9000
Price: 250 pounds sterling to 500 pounds sterling plus VAT. The price depends on the level of support required.
Notes: HEADSET combines the editing and variable length capabilities of word processor with the field-oriented structure required for most text information storage and retrieval systems. Field sizes are user-defined and over 32,000 characters per field are permitted. Other features include: repeating fields; data carry over from one record to the next; automatic generation of dates and sequential numbers; immediate validation of fields and records, and selective of full printing for proof-reading. HEADSET may be interfaced with the formats of numerous other software packages and databases using HEADFORM.
Descriptors: Data entry; word processing

HIGHSMITH CIRCULATION SYSTEM

Supplier: Highsmith Co Inc
Box 25, Fort Atkinson, WI 53538, USA
Hardware: Apple IIe; Apple III
Requirements: 5 or 10 Mb disk
Price: From 2500 to 7300 pounds sterling
Notes: Approximately 8000 borrowers
Descriptors: Issue system

I

Supplier: Information Systems Design
23 Arthur Road, Erdington, Birmingham, B24 9EX, UK
Tel: 021 384 1524
Hardware: Apricot; Sirius
Price: 295 pounds sterling
Notes: An information retrieval system which permits variable length storage of fields and records. 256,000 records may be stored, and each record may contain up to 255 fields. There are user defined formats for data input, display and printing, and 7 indexing options including full text indexing subject to user defined stoplist, keyword and name. Index updating may be online or batch. Data entry is performed in response to user defined prompts. Searching may be performed by entering a search statement ranging from a single keyword to a Boolean expression up to 4 lines long. Nested parentheses and right hand truncation are supported. Search results may be saved and sorted on up to 10 keys prior to printing.
Descriptors: Databases: inhouse; information retrieval

I&D SOFTWARE

Supplier: Genesys GMBH
PO Box 19, D-8062 Markt Indersdorf, W. Germany
Tel: 08136/7061; tlx: 527570 gesys d
Operating System: UNIX; MS DOS; PC DOS; CCP-M 2.0; DEDOS 3.1
Hardware: IBM PC; IBM PC compatibles, Siemens PC 750
Price: 1500 DM basic version; 2600 DM incl x.25 software
Notes: Genesys I&D SOFTWARE is a system designed for online information retrieval with microcomputers. The basic version of the software allows micro-to-micro and micro-to-mainframe communication also using asynchronous and x.25 links to packet switched networks. The user can define a variety of communication and terminal parameters such as baud rate, word length, parity and the effect of the break function. Features also included: functions for the preparation of online input using a standard text editing program; the preparation and storage of search profiles; uploading and downloading, and the post processing of search results. The I+D GRAPHICS SOFTWARE permits the post processing of downloaded search results containing both graphic and textual data (tektronix 4010). The extended versions of the software include communications links for packet switched networks, mainframe dependent links and the appropriate terminal emulators as for example 3270 terminals. The programs are menu driven and contain a help function.
Descriptors: Communications; graphics; online search aid; word processing

I-CIRC

Supplier: Information Systems Design
23 Arthur Road, Erdington, Birmingham, B24 9EX, UK
Tel: 021-384-1524
Operating System: MS DOS 2.11
Hardware: Apricot; Sirius
Price: 1250 + pounds sterling (including training)
Notes: An integrated system which consists of the "I" database and a version of CIRC which accesses bibliographic records from "I". The menus of both packages are amended to facilitate swapping between functions. It is suited to the library in which circulation control is a minor but nevertheless important activity. Offline recording of circulation transactions can be used while searches are performed. Overdues can be generated automatically and statistics maintained. Printouts of the catalogue, or selected sections of it, may be generated.
Descriptors: Catalogues; issue system

ILL FORMS PRINTER

Supplier: Mack Memorial Health Sciences Library, FAO Nancy Fazzone, Director
Salem Hospital, 81 Highland Avenue, Salem, MA 01970, USA
Hardware: Apple II Plus; Apple IIe; Apple III
Requirements: 48K RAM dual disk drives and printer

Price: From 20 to 125 US dollars
Notes: Produces interlibrary loans forms
Descriptors: Interlibrary loans

INDEX EDITOR
Supplier: Harley M. Templeton
7807 Lazy Lane, Austin, TX 78757, USA
Tel: 512 453 3113
Hardware: IBM PC; TI Professional
Price: 175 US dollars
Notes: The INDEX EDITOR is an index generating program. Each entry is limited to 79 characters, expandable to 117 characters when the program combines page numbers.
Review: Fetters, L.K. A guide to seven indexing programs... Database December 1985 pp 31-38
Descriptors: Indexes

INDEX PREPARATION SYSTEM
Supplier: Foxon-Maddocks Associates
10807 Oldfield Drive, Reston, VA 22091, USA
Tel: 703 476 4860
Hardware: IBM PC; IBM PC XT; IBM PC compatibles; AT+T PC
Requirements: 128K RAM; two double sided disk drives or 1 floppy and 1 hard disk drive
Price: 300 US dollars
Notes: This program creates indexes and glossaries. Index entries are limited to 600 characters each, but this can be expanded if necessary. Glossary entries may be 1500 characters long. The program can handle 2,500 records on a floppy disk system or 32,767 with a 5 Mb hard disk. Sorting is performed letter by letter or word by word and non-sort characters or phrases can be marked. The program comes with a shareware word processor capable of handling the IBM's alternate character set. Indexes may be merged or cumulated.
Review: Fetters, Linda: A guide to seven indexing programs... Database, December 1985 pp31-38
Descriptors: Indexes; word processing

INDEXING
Supplier: Mr Craig
209 Nelson Court East, Madison, TN 37115, USA
Hardware: TRS 80 Model II
Price: On application
Notes: Provides a customised list of the library's holdings of collections in areas such as: plays, short stories etc.
Descriptors: Bibliographies

INFOBASE
Supplier: Information Services, Control Data Ltd
179/199 Shaftesbury Avenue, London, WC2H 8AR, UK
Tel: 01 240 3400
Operating System: CP M; CP M-86
Hardware: Altos; Control data CD 110; DEC Rainbow; IBM PC; Rair; Sirius; Superbrain; Televideo; Torch
Descriptors: Databases: inhouse; information retrieval

INFOKOM
Supplier: Information und Kommunikation, Dietrich Rieth
Hartmann von Aue Strasse 9, 7801 Au bei Freiburg, W. Germany
Tel: 0761 407543
Operating System: PC DOS (1.1 to 3.0)
Hardware: IBM PC
Price: INFODRAW PRINT 100 US dollars; INFOMERGE 140 US dollars; INFOHIGH BOLD 150 US dollars; INFOMOUSE 210 US dollars; INFOSORT 230 US dollars; INFODOWN 290 US dollars; INFOUP 290 US dollars; INFOGRAPH 290 US dollars; INFOTEXT WORD 400 US dollars; INFOLOG 500 US dollars; INFOBANK MIRABILIS 700 US dollars
Notes: An integrated information and documentation workstation with a number of modules. INFOLOG is a communication module allowing communications with other PCs, electronic mail, file uploading, automatic logon and downloading. INFOTEXT WORD provides conventional word processing, and may be used for the preparation and post editing of searches. INFOMOUSE may be used for post editing, and is an optional feature of INFOTEXT WORD. German and English versions are available. INFOHIGH BOLD allows the user to designate certain descriptors to be highlighted immediately on the screen and boldfaced during subsequent printing. INFOGRAPH allows the user to access graphical databases, download graphics, browse and print out results during communication. May be used in conjunction with INFOLOG or as a stand alone workstation. INFODRAW PRINT permits browsing in downloaded graphics files and the printing from them. It must be used in conjunction with INFOGRAPH. INFOBANK MIRABILIS is a database management system. The program module INFODOWN allows results from online searches to be downloaded to local INFOBANK databases. INFOUP enables the transfer of information from the INFOBANK. INFOSORT permits the sorting of results of database searches according to 2 parameters, providing that the documents from various databanks contain recognisable field labels or are provided with such labels. INFOMERGE allows the user to put the search results from widely differing databanks into the same layout.
Descriptors: Electronic mail; graphics; information retrieval; online search aid; word processing

INFOQUEST
Supplier: UTLAS Corp.
701 Westchester Avenue, Suite 308W, White Plains, New York 10604, USA
Tel: (914) 997-149516; tlx: 646737
Notes: See other entry

INFOQUEST
Supplier: UTLAS Inc
80 Bloor Street West, 2nd Floor, Toronto, Ontario, Canada M5S 2V1
Tel: (416) 923 0890; tlx: 065-24479
Operating System: PC DOS
Hardware: IBM PC; IBM PC AT
Requirements: Tallgrass hard disk
Notes: Online public access catalogue and circulation modules for up to 25,000 titles. Libraries build their

files on the UTLAS Catalogue Support System (CATSS), and these records are then transferred to the library's hard disk storage device. The OPAC module offers access by author, title, subject, call number, ISBN, LCCN and UTLAS central number. Truncated search terms may be used. Authority control is available and online instructions are provided. The circulation module may be purchased with the OPAC or added later. Features include issue, discharge and renewal of items, and the generation of statistical information. Supports up to 25,000 titles
Review: Campbell, B. Infoquest: An online catalogue for small libraries. Library Hi Tech 7 1984 pp41-48
Descriptors: Catalogues; catalogues: online; issue system

INFORONICS

Supplier: Information Inc
550 Newton Road, Littleton, MA 04160, USA
Notes: Produces keyword lists to documents and text
Descriptors: Indexes

INMAGIC BIBLIO

Supplier: Head Computers Ltd
Oxted Mill, Spring Lane, Oxted, Surrey, RH8 9PB, UK
Tel: 08833 7057/5580; tlx: 957525 oxmill g
Operating System: CP M; CP M-86; MS DOS; PC DOS
Notes: Based on INMAGIC. BIBLIO is a special library applications package. Data structures and report forms for ordering, cataloguing, serials control and circulation functions are designed.
Descriptors: Acquisitions; catalogues; information retrieval; issue system; serials control

INMAGIC MICRO

Supplier: Inmagic Inc
238 Broadway, Cambridge, MA 02139, USA
Tel: 617 661 8124; tlx: 709543
Notes: See other entry

INMAGIC MICRO

Supplier: Head Computers Ltd
Oxted Mill, Spring Lane, Oxted, Surrey, RH8 9PB, UK
Tel: 08833 7057/5580; tlx: 957525 oxmill g
Operating System: CP M; CP M-86; MS DOS; PC DOS
Price: 490 pounds sterling to 880 pounds sterling for CP/M-80, 880 pounds sterling to 1270 pounds sterling for MS/PC DOS and CP/M-86. Prices are exclusive of VAT. They vary according to the level of support required.
Notes: Databases may be designed by establishing a database structure and size, as well as styles required for printed reports. The system prompts the user to name and describe the database and its contents. To build the database, the user is prompted for the information for each field in a record, and there is no limit on record length. Fields are of variable length. Boolean searching, truncation and range searching are possible. Search results may be stored for combining with another search, later printing or modification of the search strategy. Search results may be sorted by any indexed field and printed. Online updating of the database is possible. An evaluation version called TESTMAGIC is now available at 60 pounds sterling which will be deducted from the price of the INMAGIC software if this is subsequently purchased. Version 7 with full screen editor, password security at field 1 function level, calculations in reports and improved report generator is now available.
Review: Lundeen, G. and Tenopir, C. Microcomputer software for in-house databases (four top packages under 2000 pound sterling). Online 9(5) 1985, pp 30-38.
Descriptors: Databases: inhouse; information retrieval

INNOVACQ

Supplier: UTLAS Corp
701 Westchester Avenue, Suite 308W, White Plains, New York 10604, USA
Tel: (914) 997-1495; tlx: 646 737
Notes: See other entry

INNOVACQ

Supplier: UTLAS Inc
80 Bloor Street West, 2nd Floor, Toronto, Ontario, Canada, M55 2VI
Tel: (416) 923-0890; tlx: 065-24479
Notes: See other entry

INNOVACQ

Supplier: Innovative Interfaces Inc
2131 University Avenue, Suite 334, Berkeley, California 94704, USA
Hardware: Innovacq multi processor computer
Price: From 46400 US dollars, including hardware
Notes: Automated acquisition system providing: ordering; claiming; fund accounting; management reports; tracing of in process records and search capabilities. Links with bibliographic utilities and local catalogue and circulation systems are available. Serials control offers: acquisitions; fund control; claiming by issue; check in; routing; binding and label printing. Turnkey system supporting up to 30 terminals. Integrates with the UTLAS database. (See INFOQUEST)
Descriptors: Acquisitions; catalogues; catalogues: online; issue system; orders: online; serials control

INSTANTCOM ESL

Supplier: Instantcom Xworld
15110 S.W. Boones Ferry Road, Lake Oswego, OR 97034, USA
Operating System: PC DOS 2.0+
Hardware: IBM PC; IBM PC XT; IBM PC compatibles
Requirements: 128K RAM and minimum 1 floppy disk drive. 2 floppy disk drives or 1 floppy and 1 hard disk are recommended. An asynchronous communication adaptor board and a modem are required
Price: 120 US dollars with 35 dollars discount when opening Easylink account via Instant Information Inc.
Notes: ESL main module supports messaging (electronic mail and telex sending and receiving) via Western Union's Easylink Service, and information retrieval via the 'infact' service. Additional module supports communication and information retrieval with most features of Instantcom Xworld.

Review: MILLER, R. "Designing your own low cost front-end software" Online, March 1985, pp 94-98
Descriptors: Communications; electronic mail; online search aid; word processing

INSTANTCOM 3.1

Supplier: Instantcom Xworld
15110 S.W. Boones Ferry Road, Lake Oswego, OR 97034, USA
Operating System: PC DOS 2.0+
Hardware: IBM PC; IBM PC XT; IBM PC compatibles
Requirements: 128K RAM and at least 1 floppy disk drive. A configuration of 2 floppy disk drives or 1 floppy and 1 hard disk is recommended. An asynchronous communication adaptor board and a modem are required.
Price: 120 US dollars
Notes: Software for information retrieval, electronic mail and similar data transmission between a microcomputer and remotely located mainframe computers. It offers: offline preparation and disk storage of queries; automatic logon; and, when online, automatic execution of searches. Downloading, editing, additions and the transfer to other systems are also possible. Retrieved information can be printed while online or afterwards. Includes word processor, capacity for binary file transfer.
Review: Stigleman, S. "INSTANTCOM: for online communications". Online Review 8 (6) Dec 1984 pp539-42 Miller, R. "Designing your own low cost front-end software" Online, March 1985, pp 94-98.
Descriptors: Communications; electronic mail; information retrieval; online search aid; word processing

INTEGRATED MICROCOMPUTER LIBRARY SYSTEM

Supplier: Lothlorien Software
GPO Box 1033, Sydney 2001, Australia
Tel: 02 398 4122
Hardware: Apple IIe
Requirements: 11 or 20 Mb hard disk; light pen, modem optional
Price: 4000 to 6000 Australian dollars
Notes: Provides a complete circulation system, catalogue, on-line information retrieval, both at librarian and public access level and overdues control. Modem communication link is provided primarily for on-line systems software support but can also be used to link to external data and catalogue bases. It also allows external users access (read only) to the library catalogue. Acquisitions, equipment management and music/special collection management is also available. Library size: from 5,000-120,000 items with associated borrowers files. Aimed at primary and secondary schools and the smaller tertiary colleges as well as firm and special libraries.
Descriptors: Acquisitions; audio visual control; catalogues; catalogues: online; issue system; school libraries; online search aid

IT: INFORMATION TRANSFER PROGRAM

Supplier: Userlink Communications Ltd
9, Brabyns Brow, Marple, Stockport, Cheshire, SK6 7DA, UK
Tel: 061 429 8232
Operating System: PC DOS; CP M; VMS; UNIX
Hardware: IBM PC XT; Superbrain; VAX; U 750; U 780
Requirements: IBM PC XT 256K RAM, Superbrain 64K RAM and 720K disk storage
Notes: The IT system provides the intelligence needed to carry out an online search. All the procedures needed to use a communications network and send commands to an information retrieval system are coded into a program which carries out all these actions automatically for ordinary users. System features include natural language dialogue with the user, a tutorial session to explain the entry of information sources and search execution. There is an automatic re-entry system in the event of connection difficulties, and advice on action if the search is not successful. Storage of search strategies on disk for re-use and the collection of output from the remote computer for later printing are also possible.
Descriptors: Online search aid

KAMBIS

Supplier: Karmac B.V.
PO BOX 212, 8200 AE Lelystad, The Netherlands
Tel: 03200 44244; tlx: 70110 karto nl
Operating System: PC DOS
Hardware: IBM PC; IBM PC XT; IBM PC AT
Requirements: 256-512K RAM, 5364 driver card, 40-80 Mb disk and 5.25" floppy disk drive, 4 local work stations
Price: 55,000 Dfl
Notes: The software package allows cataloguing, acquisitions, serials control, membership registration, circulation control, payroll, accounting, reports and statistics to be integrated in one system. The acquisitions module permits the ordering, receipt, claiming and cancellation of items as well as producing management and financial reports. The cataloguing function is completely based on ISBD rules and allows searching on subject, author, title, serial, genre, ISBN and collection. The circulation control module uses a high-volume transaction barcode scanner which may be used as a stand-alone device, or with a light pen barcode reader. All transactions concerning fines, renewals, acquisitions and reservations are monitored, and the statistics module provides detailed analyses of the usage of the collection.
Descriptors: Acquisitions; catalogues; catalogues: online; issue system; serials control

KWIRS

Supplier: Norman Paton
21 Airyhall Gardens, Aberdeen, AB1 7QL, UK
Tel: 0224 36130
Operating System: Applesoft
Hardware: Apple II
Price: 18 pounds sterling
Notes: Provides for detailed analytical indexing of information materials for school and college libraries
Descriptors: Catalogues; information retrieval

LASS

Supplier: Sashalom Pty Ltd
4th Floor, APA Building, 53 Martin Place, Sydney 2000, Australia
Operating System: Datapoint DOS; Wicat MCS
Requirements: Minimum 1 Mb disk for every 1,000 books; 132 column printer; Datashare interpreter with Datapoint DOS; Datacat interpreter with Wicat MCS
Price: 2200 Australian dollars
Notes: Library system designed for use by solicitors. Indexes author, title catalogue number and subject keywords. LASS also controls loans and prints accessions and holding lists.
Descriptors: Accessions lists; catalogues; issue system; law libraries

LAWTERM

Supplier: Legal Technology Group
58 South Eaton Place, London, SW1W 9JJ, UK
Tel: 01 730 8040
Hardware: BBC
Requirements: Full duplex modem
Price: Less than 200 pounds sterling with modem
Notes: Aids online access to EUROLEX. Access to LAWTERM which operates at 1200/75 baud is under development.
Descriptors: Online access to Eurolex; law libraries

LENDING LIBRARY (THE)

Supplier: G & G Software Ltd
The Old Cider House, Golant, Fowey, Cornwall, PL23 1LN, UK
Tel: 072683 2315
Operating System: MS DOS; UNIX
Hardware: No specific model
Price: 6000 pounds sterling (large discounts for education). Hardware prices available on request
Notes: Performs all normal housekeeping functions: issue, return, renewal, reservations, overdues, reservation notices, periodical receipts and circulation lists and departmental budgeting. The catalogue caters for books, periodicals and abstracts. Indexes are produced for all major fields. Full search facilities are offered using and/or combinations. Size is limited only by database capacity: 20,000 books and 2,000 borrowers on a 20 MB disk; 500,000 books and 10,000 borrowers on a 120 MB disk. Number of users also hardware limited, eg Cifer, 6 users, Honeywell, 16 users.
Descriptors: Catalogues; catalogues: online; issue system

LIAISON

Supplier: Captec, Computer Applied Techniques Ltd.
3 St James Terrace, Malahide, Co Dublin, Ireland
Tel: 353 1 450921; tlx: 31432 fjk ei; Eurokom Fred Kennedy; Eirmail 74: EIM158
Operating System: MS DOS
Hardware: IBM PC; Olivetti M 24
Notes: Features include: automatic log on and off; an audiovisual option; interactive communications; transaction recording; terminal emulation; file transfer and document delivery. The baud rate can be selected between 110 and 9600. The edit function may be used while the micro is running in receiving mode. Many features are provided through use of single keystrokes.
Descriptors: Communications; online search aid

LIBRAFILE

Supplier: H.W. Bookservice
227 Stanley Road, Bootle, Merseyside, L20 3DY, UK
Operating System: OS 1.2
Hardware: BBC
Requirements: Disk drive and printer
Price: 18.60 pounds sterling (disk); 29 pounds sterling (ROM)
Notes: A loans management system for the junior, middle or secondary school library. Features the automatic calculation of return dates, automatically printed overdue reminders and on screen cues for books on the reserved list. The program is menu driven. Each data disk of 100K can hold up to 400 records. Lists books on loan by form, group, book title, author, etc.
Descriptors: Issue system; school libraries

LIBRAFILE: BARCODE VERSION

Supplier: H.W. Bookservice
227 Stanley Road, Bootle, Merseyside, L20 3DY, UK
Operating System: OS 1.2
Hardware: BBC
Requirements: Double sided twin disk 400-800K, printer, MEP barcode reader
Price: 37.20 pounds sterling
Notes: Library loans management for the junior, middle or secondary school. Prints barcoded reader tickets and book labels. Records of pupils and book loans from the school library may be kept on disk, and 1,500 pupil records and 400 book records per 100K disk are supported. Overdue reminders are automatically printed. Input may be either via the keyboard or from the barcode reader.
Descriptors: Issue system; school libraries

LIBRAMATIX

Supplier: Pragmatix Pty Ltd
66 Berry Street, North Sydney, NSW 2060, Australia
Operating System: CP M-86; CCP M-86; MS DOS; PC DOS
Requirements: 128K RAM, dual floppy disk drives, and printer
Price: 600 Australian dollars
Notes: A record retrieval, sorting and report writing system that can handle up to 50,000 titles. Titles can be retrieved by title, author, ISBN, date of publication, abstract, language, subject or up to 10 concatonated keywords. Reports are formatted by the user.
Descriptors: Bibliographies; catalogues; reference management

LIBRARIAN

Supplier: Equinox Computers
16 Anning Street, New Inn Yard, London EC2A 3HB, UK
Tel: 01 729 4460; tlx: 27341
Notes: See other entry

LIBRARIAN

Supplier: Eurotec Consultants Ltd
143 Hythe Hill, Colchester, Essex, CO1 2NF, UK
Tel: 0206 572538
Operating System: CCP M-86; Concurrent DOS
Price: From 1450 pounds sterling per module plus VAT
Notes: LIBRARIAN is an integrated library administration system currently incorporating: cataloguing; online public access, and circulation control. Catalogue entries are designed to the requirements of each library, as too are the enquiry access points (eg author, title word, subject, classification, ISBN, year of publication, etc. which may be combined using the Boolean operators AND, OR and NOT). Circulation control information is also user-defined, particularly material/borrower categories and fine/penalty systems. Transactions are barcode driven with a secure audit trail. Public enquirers obtain current loan status/availability of any material which results from an enquiry. Reserved material availability and overdue notices are readily produced. Usage statistics relating to both material and borrowers are automatically maintained by the system. Each module within LIBRARIAN is menu-driven, requiring only single-key responses. Data entry and amendments are via a simple, form-filling procedure with full editing facilities. Output can be sent to the screen, printer, or disk. Disk output is in a word-processing compatible format. There are no size limitations in the system. Storage capacity is limited only by the amount of hard disk available.
Review: Library Micromation News (3) (Jan 1984) pp7-14; The Law Librarian, 14 (3), December
Descriptors: Catalogues; catalogues: online; information retrieval; issue system

LIBRARY ACCOUNTS

Supplier: Edinburgh University Library in conjunction with Edinburgh Regional Computing centre.
Medical Library, Edinburgh, Edinburgh University, Edinburgh, UK
Hardware: Apple II; Sirius
Requirements: UCSD pascal
Notes: Not commercially available, but cost-sharing considered. Provides for library expenditure, for example, staff travel, binding costs, book funds and serials expenditure.
Descriptors: Finances

LIBRARY BUDGET FTE CALC

Supplier: Leicester Polytechnic Library
PO Box 143, Leicester, LE1 9BH, UK
Tel: 0533 551551
Hardware: Commodore pet
Price: 8 pounds sterling per module
Notes: Uses student numbers and average stock prices to calculate library budget
Review: Adams, R., Library budget: a computer program in "BASIC" Leicester Polytechnic Library, 1982
Descriptors: Finances

LIBRARY CIRCULATION MANAGER

Supplier: K 12 Micromedia Publishing
6 Arrow Road, Ramsey, NJ 07446, USA
Tel: (201) 825-8888
Hardware: Apple II; TRS 80 model II; TRS 80 model III
Requirements: 32K RAM, disk drive and 80 column printer
Price: 199 US dollars
Notes: Developed for small school libraries. Records information for 300 students borrowing up to 6 books each (2 disk drives can accommodate up to 800 students)
Descriptors: Issue system; school libraries

LIBRARY CIRCULATION SYSTEM II

Supplier: Winnebago Software Co.
121 SO. Marshall Caledonia, MN 55921, USA
Operating System: Pro DOS
Hardware: Apple IIe; Apple IIc; Apple II Plus
Requirements: 2 floppy disk drives and a printer. Apple IIc needs 64K RAM
Price: 895.00 US dollars
Notes: Full circulation program designed for the multi-media library includes inventory. Handles 60,000 materials, 3,500 users.
Descriptors: Issue system

LIBRARY CIRCULATION SYSTEM III

Supplier: Winnebago Software Co.
121 SO. Marshall Caledonia, MN 55921, USA
Operating System: DOS 3.3
Hardware: Apple IIe
Requirements: Corvus or Sider hard disk, 2 floppy disk drives, and a printer
Price: 995.00 US dollars
Notes: Full circulation program designed for the multi-media library on a hard disk, includes inventory. Handles 60,000 items, 5,000 users.
Descriptors: Issue system

LIBRARY HELPER OVERDUES

Supplier: Southern Micro Systems
PO Box 2097, Burlington, NC 27216-2097, USA
Tel: 929 226 7610, 800 334 5521
Hardware: Apple II Plus; Apple IIe; Apple IIc
Requirements: Printer
Price: 69 US dollars; 29 US dollars for additional disks
Notes: A record-keeping system which will: list all overdues; print overdue notices; print fine notices; print forgetter's list; sort; search; edit, add and delete records. 300 students may be listed per disk. The program includes complete instructions, documentation and two disks (one for back up).

Descriptors: Overdues

LIBRARY MANAGEMENT SYSTEM

Supplier: Top Systems Ltd, fao Benny Segal
Attn. 237020, B Wilson Street, Tel-Aviv, 65220, Israel
Operating System: MS DOS; Infoshare (novell)
Notes: LMS was designed for the management of libraries and information centres and was developed in Israel by Top Systems Ltd and Triple D Micro software Ltd. It may be operated as a single-user, multi-user or networked system. The system was developed using screen and report generators which enable it to be customised to run application programs in any languages, such as French, Dutch, Swedish etc. or to suit a particular application. It offers the following features: inventory information, lending reports, circulation and check-in, vendor information, circulation lists, searches, keywords and thesaurus, mailing lists. See also CALM.
Descriptors: acquisitions; catalogues; issue system; serials control; thesaurus control

LIBRARY MATE (previously Librarian)

Supplier: Geoglobal Systems, Inc
Marketing Division, 5296 Butternut E., Columbus, Ohio, OH 43229, USA
Operating System: Apple DOS 3.3
Hardware: Apple II; Apple IIc; Apple II Plus; Apple III
Price: 180 US dollars
Notes: General purpose database management system with keyword retrieval capabilities and Boolean logic. The records can each hold up to 700 characters of information, and about 125 of these maximum-sized records will fit on a single 5.25" disk with 300 average-sized records per disk. Sorting is possible and many different output formats may be designed. A record may include any number of keywords, providing these fit within the record size selected by the user. Several report formats are provided. LIBRARY MATE is being used for a wide range of applications including cataloguing.
Review: Garten, E.D. Library Mate: database with keyword indexing. The Electronic Library 2 (4) October 1984 pp242-243 and Library Hi Tech
Descriptors: Databases: inhouse; indexes; information retrieval

LIBRARY MICROTOOLS: OVERDUES

Supplier: K 12 Micromedia Publishing
6 Arrow Road, Ramsey, NJ 07446, USA
Tel: (201) 825-8888
Price: 49 US dollars plus 5
Notes: For use with PFS, LIBRARY MICROTOOLS: OVERDUES is a predesigned form to handle library overdues. Records contain: teacher, student, grade, title, author, call no, date due, price and comment, and reports may be produced by: student, teacher, grade, notices or title searches. Each disk will accomodate approximately 500 records.
Descriptors: Overdues; school libraries

LIBRARY MONITOR

Supplier: Colorado Computer West
PO Box 206, Kremmling, CO 80459, USA
Operating System: DOS 3.3
Hardware: Apple II Plus
Requirements: 48K RAM, dual disk drives and a printer
Price: 250 US dollars
Notes: School library overdue system. Capacity for up to 1600 entries with up to 500 overdues.
Descriptors: Overdues; school libraries

LIBRARY QUIZ

Supplier: Media Center Factory
PO Box 13536, Greensboro, NC 27405, USA
Hardware: Apple II; Apple II Plus; Apple IIe; TRS 80 model I; TRS 80 model III; TRS 80 model IV
Price: 15 US dollars
Notes: Offers multiple choice questions
Descriptors: User education

LIBRARY SEARCH AND SOLVE

Supplier: K 12 Micromedia Publishing
6 Arrow Road, Ramsey, NJ 07446, USA
Tel: (201)825-8888
Hardware: Apple
Price: 29.95 US dollars plus 5
Notes: LIBRARY SEARCH AND SOLVE uses both the micro and the library's own resources in a picture puzzle-solving context to enable students to become skilful in using the reference materials in the media centre. Students work independently at their own rate, using animated graphics; a high scorers' hall of fame and a certificate of merit provide incentive. Teachers can add their own questions and hints or use those supplied.
Descriptors: User education

LIBRARY SKILLS

Supplier: K 12 Micromedia Publishing
6 Arrow Road, Ramsey, NJ, 07446, USA
Tel: (201) 825-8888
Hardware: Apple
Price: 42 US dollars
Notes: Intended for use in school libraries. Students are introduced to the card catalogue, the three basic catalogue cards, the title page and the parts of the book.
Descriptors: School libraries; User education

LIBRARY SKILLS: RIGHT ON

Supplier: Right On Programs
PO Box 977, Huntingdon, NY 11743, USA
Hardware: Apple II Plus; Apple IIe; Commodore pet; Commodore 64
Requirements: Commodore pet 32K RAM
Price: 18 US dollars
Notes: 12 programs designed for use in school libraries including using the catalogue, the Dewey Decimal Classification, use of contents pages etc.
Descriptors: School libraries; user education

LIBRARY USAGE SKILLS
Supplier: JMC Computer Service Inc
1005 West Elm Street, Lake City, Minnesota 55041, USA
Hardware: Apple II
Requirements: 48K RAM and disk drive
Price: 74 US dollars
Notes: Self-instructional tutorial at three levels of difficulty: 1. Upper elementary, includes classification, card catalogue and reference. 2. Junior high, includes classification, card catalogue, reader's guide and reference. 3. Senior high, includes card catalogue, reader's guide and reference.
Descriptors: School libraries; user education

LIBS 100: SYSTEM 23
Supplier: CLSI Ltd (UK)
Regent Arcade House, 252-260 Regent Street, London, W1R 5DA, UK
Tel: 01 437 8090
Notes: See other entry

LIBS 100: SYSTEM 23
Supplier: CLSI Inc
1220 Washington Street, West Newton, MA 02165, USA
Tel: 617 965 6310
Hardware: DEC LSI 11 23
Requirements: 256K RAM, DEC compatible RH11 disk controller, communications equipment for up to 16 terminals
Notes: An integrated library system, system 23 can handle all the libs 100 software previously available on larger processors only. This includes the complete libs 100 circulation control application, the public access catalogue, the acquisitions module and the materials booking module. Specialised software modules are also available including the TCOM interface facility, the reserve book room module, the networking module and the MARC input tape facility. The library may use all of these modules or only a few, adding as required.
Descriptors: Acquisitions; catalogues: online; issue system; MARC interface

LICON
Supplier: Graham Wheater and Son Ltd
12 Churchill Road, Canterbury, Kent, CT1 3EB, UK
Tel: 0227 457232
Notes: See other entry

LICON
Supplier: Licon Systems
6 Hillview Road, Rayleigh, Essex, S96 7HX, UK
Tel: 0268 770740
Operating System: PC DOS; MS DOS; Netware
Hardware: IBM PC XT; IBM PC AT; IBM PC compatibles
Requirements: May be used with Novell S or G network systems for a multi-user environment
Price: Single user 2,250 pounds sterling
Notes: LICON is a library management system with facilities for circulation control, catalogues and book ordering. The circulation functions take place from one screen which is split into two main sections: one to display borrower details and the other to display book details. Single key depressions are used throughout to perform the function selected. Statistical data on the frequency of borrower library usage and the frequency of book issues are incorporated into the system. Supplier and order details are maintained within the system and, when a book is received, its details can be transferred to the catalogue file without rekeying. The catalogue record has fields for up to two authors, accession number, ISBN, Dewey classification, full title, title key words, publisher, general notes and status information. Books may be displayed or printed in a variety of sequences or a search may be made on selected parts of the records and the results displayed.
Descriptors: Acquisitions; catalogues; catalogues: online; issue system

LIDAS
Supplier: Central Management Library, FAO Stephen Hume
Management and Personnel Office, Whitehall, London, SW1A 2AZ, UK
Tel: 01 273 5788
Requirements: Any microcomputer to act as a terminal
Notes: Serials control system on bureau with Comshare Ltd. Data entry via microcomputer planned.
Descriptors: Serials control

LINX
Supplier: Faxon Europe
Nieuwezijds Voorburgwal 60, 1012 SC Amsterdam
Tel: 020-24 08 85
Notes: See other entry.

LINX
Supplier: Faxon
15 Southwest Park, Westwood, MA 02090, USA
Tel: 800 225 6055
Requirements: Any microcomputer which can act as a terminal
Price: On application
Notes: Online, remote access system, including routing system and union list capability. Micro used as intelligent terminal. See also MICROLINX check-in.
Review: IRELAND, Jeanetta M. "Faxon LINX at Brandei's University Libraries: a user's appraisal". Lib Hi Tech 2 (1) 1984 pp29-35
Descriptors: Acquisitions; circulation: serials; orders: online; serials control

LIS
Supplier: Georgetown University Medical Center
Washington DC, 20007, USA
Operating System: MUMPS
Hardware: DEC 11 23 series; DEC 11 73 series
Price: 45,000 to 55,000 US dollars. Capital outlay for start up to run LIS on 11/23 seires under 50,000 US dollars range.
Notes: A total system consisting of acquisitions, cataloguing, circulation and serials modules. The system

is menu driven with one entry point. The acquisitions module uses an interface with OCLC to download MARC records at the time of ordering. This record is updated after receipt to complete the cataloguing record and the item record for circulation. The online catalogue has author, title, subject and keyword approaches, and allows Boolean searching and truncation. Computer Output Microfilm is available as a backup to the online catalogue. Medical libraries may use the NLM MeSH vocabulary online as the subject authority. LC headings may be entered. Circulation is based on borrower, item and barcode files. The system also supports networking with interlibrary loans, accounting, word processing and the miniMEDLINE system (an end user bibliographic search system based on a subset of MEDLINE).
Review: Broering, N.C. "An affordable microcomputer library and information system developed by Georgetown University". Microcomputers for Information Management 1 (4) Dec 1984 pp269-283
Descriptors: Acquisitions; catalogues; catalogues: online; interlibrary loans; information retrieval: commercial database subsets; issue system; medical libraries; serials control; word processing

LITER
Supplier: USDA SEA, FAO John D. Ross
Water Quality Management Laboratory,
Durant, OK 74701, USA
Hardware: Wang 2200C
Price: No price available
Notes: Controls up to 99,999 references (single disk maximum 1020). Index terms may be searched, combined with Boolean logic.
Review: Ross, J.D. "LITER: a LITERature reference information retrieval program". Agricultural Engineering 60 (10) November 1979, pp16-17
Descriptors: Information retrieval; reference management

LOAN
Supplier: Computerland Stores
PO Box 31098, Phoenix, AZ 85046, USA
Hardware: Apple II
Requirements: 48K RAM and specialised communications hardware and software
Price: 2500 US dollars or 'free' with hardware
Notes: Interlibrary loan network for regional library services, also supporting electronic mail, bulletin board service and automatic call and answering. Maximum storage 500,000 characters. May be used with Nestar Cluster Drive System with up to 64 Apple II's and up to 33 Mb storage.
Review: Rorvig, M.E. Microcomputers and libraries: a guide to technology, products and applications. New York, Knowledge Industry Publications, 1981. ISBN 0-914236-67-9, pp48-9
Descriptors: Bulletin board; electronic mail; interlibrary loans

LSSI LASERFILE SYSTEM
Supplier: Library Systems and Services, Inc
1395 Piccard Drive, Suite 100, Rockville, MD 20850, USA
Tel: 1 800 638 8725
Operating System: PC DOS
Hardware: IBM PC
Price: On application
Notes: LASERFILE (TM) is a database system using laser readable video discs to enhance and upgrade a library's conversion and cataloguing needs, enabling large public and academic libraries to operate massive storage and retrieval systems onsite and online. The system consists of a laser disc player, controller and PC interface. Each laser disc holds up to one gigabyte of information from the following databases: LC MARC; GPO; REMARC; NICEM. Up to four disc players may be used with up to six IBM PC's. A printer may be attached, enabling the production of catalogue cards or labels.
Descriptors: Catalogues; catalogues: online; information retrieval: commercial database subsets; retrospective conversion

LSTERM COMMUNICATIONS SOFTWARE
Supplier: OCLC
6565 Frantz Road, Dublin, Ohio 43017, USA
Tel: (614)764-6000
Notes: See other entry

LSTERM COMMUNICATIONS SOFTWARE
Supplier: OCLC Europe
2nd Floor, Lloyds Bank Chambers, 75 Edmund Street, Birmingham, B3 3HA, UK
Tel: 021 236 3224; tlx: 335176 oclc tfs trsg
Operating System: PC DOS
Hardware: OCLC M300 workstation; IBM PC
Notes: Enables libraries to use M300 workstations or IBM PCs as LS2000 terminals. Planned enhancements include save screen and programmable function keys.
Descriptors: Communications; electronic mail; online access to OCLC

LS2000 SERIALS CONTROL
Supplier: OCLC
6565 Frantz Road, Dublin, Ohio, 43017, USA
Tel: (614)764-6000
Notes: See other entry

LS2000 SERIALS CONTROL
Supplier: OCLC Europe
2nd Floor, Lloyds Bank Chambers, 75 Edmund Street, Birmingham, B3 3HA, UK
Tel: 021 236 3224; tlx: 335176 oclc tfstrsg
Operating System: PC DOS
Hardware: IBM PC; OCLC M300 workstation
Requirements: Hard disk
Notes: Integrates the new SC350 stand alone microcomputer serials subsystem. Provides bibliographic control, check in, routing, claiming, bindery control, financial control, subscription maintenance and report generation facilities. In addition to downloading bibliographic information from the OCLC Online Union Catalogue, libraries may input and maintain serials information on the micro, transfer information to the OCLC online system for union listing, and transfer summary and detailed holdings information between the micro and the LS2000

computer. See LSTERM COMMUNICATIONS SOFTWARE.
Descriptors: Serials control

MACREX

Supplier: Bayside Indexing Service
265 Arlington Avenue, Kensington, CA 94707, USA
Tel: (415) 524-4195
Price: 280-325 US dollars (depending on hardware)
Notes: See other entry

MACREX

Supplier: Calvert, AH and DME
38 Rochester Road, London, NW1 9JJ, UK
Tel: 01 267 3793
Operating System: MS DOS 2.0+; CP/M 2.2
Requirements: MS DOS - minimum 128K RAM and 1 disk drive; CP/M - minimum 64K RAM, 1 disk drive and Z80 processor
Price: 140 pounds sterling - 240 pounds sterling (280-325 US dollars) depending on hardware; extra with MICREX
Notes: Program specifically designed for book and periodical indexing from page proofs. Allows for entry, verification and editing of index items. Sorts (word-by-word or letter-by-letter) and merges multiple references automatically. Prints final copy in one of several layouts (including run-on and indented subheadings) which may be defined by user. Will also produce disk files for transfer to phototypesetter. Special codes for this purpose may be included. Special characters may be defined by the user. Input may be from ASCII file as well as keyboard. Capactiy is dependant on hardware used. Indexes in excess of 100,000 lines may be preprared on hard disk systems. See also MICREX.
Review: Recent issues of the Indexer and Microindexer; Fetters,L.K., A guide to seven indexing programs, Database, December 1985, pp 31-38
Descriptors: Indexes

MAGPIE

Supplier: Kent Barlow Information Associates
Kingsmead House, 250 Kings Road, Chelsea, London, SW3 5UE, UK
Tel: 01 351 2776; tlx: 268627
Operating System: CP M; PC DOS
Hardware: IBM PC XT
Price: 225 pounds sterling
Notes: Combines SWIFT and AQUILA and can be adapted for use with any online system. Accesses CAS online, ESA, DIMDI and Dialog. An additional clean up package is available to strip out unwanted detail, and to translate codes from the host and convert them into tags for AQUILA.
Descriptors: Information retrieval; online search aid

MARS: MICROCOMPUTER ARCHIVES AND RECORDS MANAGEMENT SYSTEMS

Supplier: East Tennessee State University C/O R.M. Kesner, Director of the Archives of Appalachia
East Tennessee State University, USA
Hardware: Apple II Plus
Requirements: 32K RAM, communicator card, dual disk drive and printer. Other micros with Basic or PASCAL on application.
Review: Kesner. R.M. Hurst, D. "Microcomputer applications in archives a study in progress" Archivaria (12) Summer 1981, pp1-19
Descriptors: Archive control

MASTER LEGAL SYSTEM PC

Supplier: Master Data Center Inc
29100 Northwestern Highway, Southfield, MI 48034, USA
Tel: 313 352 5810
Notes: See other entry

MASTER LEGAL SYSTEM PC

Supplier: Information und Kommunikation
Dietrich Rieth, Hartmann von Aue Str. 9, D-7801 Freiburg-AU, Germany
Tel: 0761 702202
Hardware: IBM PC XT
Requirements: 256K RAM, 10.7 Mb hard disk minimum plus a dual sided floppy disk drive of 360K
Notes: The system utilises a common database for patents, trade marks and general legal matters. The modular design allows the user to start with any module and add others later. System features include online data entry and updating, interactive inquiry and record display, multiple indexes allowing browsing and direct access to selected files and data, and keyword searching. The system is menu driven and includes "help" screens. There is built in multi level security that limits individuals to authorised tasks only.
Descriptors: Information retrieval; legal documentation

MCGRAW HILL INTERACTIVE AUTHORING SYSTEM

Supplier: McGraw Hill Book Company
Shoppenhanger Road, Maidenhead, Berks, SL6 2QL, UK
Tel: 0628 23431
Operating System: PC DOS
Hardware: IBM PC
Requirements: 128K RAM, 320K floppy disk drives and serial interface to video, UCSD Pascal
Price: 1495 pounds sterling for version 3.1
Notes: A librarian may use the software to create a programmed course of instruction.
Review: PC User (May 1984) pp85-90
Descriptors: User education

MEDIA AND EQUIPMENT MANAGEMENT

Supplier: Educational Activities Inc (Distributor)
1937 Grand Avenue, Baldwin, New York, 11510, USA
Hardware: Apple II Plus; Apple IIe; Commodore pet; Atari; TRS 80 model III; TRS 80 model IV
Requirements: Dual disk drives on Atari
Price: 89 US dollars each, or 325 US dollars for 4 programs
Notes: Four independent programs designed to be used together as a complete management system to control the inventory and loaning of AV equipment and materials.

Descriptors: Audio visual control

MEDICAL LIBRARIAN
Supplier: Westminster Medical Systems Ltd
PO Box 100, Cobham, Surrey, KT11 2HG, UK
Tel: 0932 68388
Hardware: ICL PC
Price: 7900+ pounds sterling plus VAT (including hardware, installation and support)
Notes: A special version of LIBRARIAN. It offers a comprehensive catalogue facility and easy to use enquiry system with access by author, subject or title. It is designed for small and medium sized medical libraries.
Descriptors: Catalogues; medical libraries

METAID
Supplier: Metascybe Systems Ltd
78 Long Lane, London, EC1A 9ET, UK
Tel: 01 606 6865/6
Operating System: CP M
Hardware: Casu super C; Casu mini
Requirements: Lyme 5000 VDU
Price: 150 pounds sterling plus
Notes: Teletype emulation enabling storage and transmission of up to 225 characters and 11 search strings and downloading to disk.
Descriptors: Online search aid

METALOGUE
Supplier: Oriel Computers
Prins Hendrikkade 22, 1012 TM Amsterdam, The Netherlands
Tel: 020 258499
Notes: Distributors for METALOGUE in Europe. For details of software see other entry.

METALOGUE
Supplier: Oriel Computer Services Ltd
Chipping Norton, Oxon, OX7 5LY, UK
Tel: 0608 41351/4; tlx: 837512 oriel g
Operating System: CP/M-86; MS DOS; PC DOS
Hardware: IBM PC; Orion; Sirius
Requirements: 8086 or 8088 based micros, minimum 256K RAM
Price: 2000 to 3000 pounds sterling depending on hardware configuration
Notes: Supports all types of book and non book materials. Simple or complex bibliographic records can be defined, input, accessed and displayed. Authority records can be constructed and any number of index sequences defined. Printed catalogues, catalogue cards and viewdata frames may be generated.
Descriptors: Catalogues; catalogues: online; viewdata

METAMICRO
Supplier: Metamicro Library Systems Inc
1818 San Pedro, San Antonio, Texas 78212, USA
Tel: 512 736 9309
Operating System: Uniflex
Hardware: SWTP S plus
Requirements: 128K RAM minimum 1,000K RAM maximum. Disk drives: 16 Mb 1 unit to 32 Mb 1 unit. 1 to 5 terminals. 1 to 3 printers.
Price: 5001 to 10,000 US dollars
Notes: Serials control system allowing cataloguing using full MARC records and searching under 12 different types of key. Check in is available with prompting for specific issues. Routing, automatic claiming, bindery control, financial control and duplicates control are features of the system. There is a print generator which will sort, allow the generation of KWIC and KWOC indexes, statistics and forms, and provide format editing and word processing facilities.
Descriptors: Indexes; serials control; word processing

MICREX
Supplier: Calvert, AH and DME
38 Rochester Road, London, NW1 9JJ, UK
Tel: 01 267 3793
Operating System: CP M
Requirements: 56K RAM and minimum 1 disk drive
Price: 75 pounds sterling (220 pounds sterling with macrex)
Notes: An indexing program which can handle about 1250 short entries or 400 long ones. Formatting features may be user defined. Entries can be retrieved and edited at any time; sorting and printing effects are possible. Files can be merged into a single Macrex file. See also MACREX.
Review: Fetters, L.K. A guide to seven indexing programs... Database December 1985 pp31-38
Descriptors: Indexes

MICRO CAIRS
Supplier: RTZ Computer Services
1 Redcliff Street, Bristol, BS99 7JS, UK
Tel: 0272 24181
Notes: See other entry

MICRO CAIRS
Supplier: Leatherhead Food Research Association
Randalls Road, Leatherhead, Surrey, KT22 7RY, UK
Operating System: CP/M-86; MS DOS
Hardware: Apricot; Eagle systems; Future technology; HP 150; IBM PC; Sirius; Texas instruments
Requirements: MICRO CAIRS will operate on other 16 bit microcomputers with Intel 8086 or 8088 processors
Price: From 600 pounds sterling
Notes: An integral information retrieval and library automation package. Permits the entry, indexing, storage and retrieval of textual or numerical information. MICRO CAIRS can provide up to 8 separate databases each with its own structure and retrieval requirements. Records can be divided into 80 fields with 2000 characters per field. Batch and online data entry, deletion, retrieval and modification are provided using user configurable screens. Indexing terms may be taken from the data fields or added manually. There is an optional thesaurus which can be used on data entry and retrieval. Inverted or sequential methods of retrieval are available. There are 26 output formats and the possibility of adding security restrictions. Bulletin production and current awareness searching are possible.

In addition, there are printed index and catalogue generation facilities.
Review: Lundeen, G. and Tenopir, C., Microcomputer software for in-house databases (four top packages under pounds sterling 2000). Online 9 (5) 1985, pp30-38.
Descriptors: Databases: inhouse; indexes; information retrieval; thesaurus control

MICRO INDEXING SYSTEM
Supplier: Compugramma Inc (Erica Mugglestone)
PO Box 60, Craubury, NJ 08512, USA
Tel: 609 448 9152
Hardware: IBM PC; IBM PC XT
Requirements: Hardware requirements: 128K RAM and one disk drive minimum. A RAM disk is recommended to decrease sorting time.
Price: 600 US dollars for the basic program, 100 US dollars for the utilities package
Notes: The program supports run-in or indented style indexes, but special formats may also be purchased. The indexer specifies the number of characters per line, the number of indentation spaces, the number of lines desired between entries and the location of cross references. Most commands may be programmed into function keys. Other facilities include: on screen editing; sorting; printing effects; and the cumulation of indexes.
Review: Fetters, L.K. A guide to seven indexing programs... Database December 1985 pp31-38
Descriptors: Indexes

MICRO QUESTEL
Notes: See TAMIL

MICRO SCAN: DISCLOSURE
Supplier: Disclosure
5161 River Road, Bethesda, MD 20816, USA
Tel: 800 638 8076
Operating System: PC DOS
Hardware: IBM PC; IBM PC XT
Notes: Software contains information on 5100 publicly traded companies. The information comes monthly on 3 disks, but if more current stock prices are needed between the monthly updates, it is possible to update the disks daily. The disks also contain a complete set of integrated software programs which allow the screening, sorting and ranking of companies, portfolio analysis and report writing, statistics, histograms and the transfer of data to spread sheets.
Descriptors: Information retrieval: commercial database subsets; statistics

MICRO SEARCH
Supplier: Eric Clearinghouse on Information Resources
030 Huntington Hall, Syracuse University, Syracuse, NY 13210, USA
Tel: (315)423 3640
Operating System: DOS 3.3
Hardware: Aplle II Plus; Apple IIe; Apple; Franklin Ace 1000
Requirements: Apple III requires emulator. All micros must have minimum 48K RAM and disk drive
Price: 6 US dollars plus 6 US dollars per disk
Notes: Floppies with subsets of the Eric database
Descriptors: Eric database subsets; information retrieval: commercial database subsets

MICRO STATUS
Supplier: AERE Harwell
Marketing and Sales Department, Bld 329, AERE Harwell, Oxon, OX11 0RA, UK
Tel: 0235 24141 x 2704; tlx: 83135
Operating System: PC DOS; UNIX
Hardware: Fortune 32:16; IBM PC XT
Requirements: Minimum 512K RAM and 10 Mb hard disk
Price: 1,500 pounds sterling single-user; 4,000 pounds sterling multi-user; 750 pounds sterling read only version.
Notes: STATUS on microcomputers offers the ability to handle a range of information from full free text to highly structured text. Boolean and proximity searching are possible, and there are comprehensive display and routing capabilities. There is no limit on size of any Article or Named Section, other than a limit on the maximum size of any file of 30Mb. MICRO STATUS offers easy interfaces to word processors, optical character readers, graphics etc. and there are comprehensive multi level security controls. May be used for inhouse databases or data downloaded from mainframes running STATUS. This information may be read by a read only version of MICRO STATUS.
Review: Information World Review, May 1986 No 4, p10
Descriptors: Databases: inhouse; information retrieval

MICROBIRD
Supplier: Technology and Law Ltd, FAO Carolyn Hayman
56 Britton Street, London EC1M 5NA, UK
Hardware: Apple IIe; DEC PDP 11; IBM PC; Onyx; Plexus; Sage IV; Sirius
Requirements: DEC PDP 11 with RSTS
Notes: A full text retrieval system designed to be used with databases which consist largely of unstructured text. Applications of MICROBIRD include: reports and correspondence; abstracts; catalogue entries; and the support for the preparation of manuals and reference documents. Documents may be entered directly to the system or may be fed in via a word processor or downloaded from other computers.
Descriptors: Databases: inhouse; information retrieval

MICROCOMPUTERISED PERIODICAL MANAGEMENT SYSTEM
Supplier: Avery International Research Center
325 North Altadena Drive, Pasadena, CA 91107, USA
Hardware: Apple IIe
Notes: Up to 600 periodicals
Descriptors: Serials control

MICROCON
Supplier: OCLC
6565 Frantz Road, Dublin, Ohio, 43017, USA
Tel: (614) 764-6000
Notes: See other entry

MICROCON

Supplier: OCLC Europe
2nd Floor, Lloyds Bank Chambers, 75
Edmund Street, Birmingham, B3 3HA, UK
Tel: 021 236 3224; tlx: 335176 oclc tfstrs g

Notes: MICROCON is a batch retrospective search service that helps libraries to obtain retrospective conversion. It enables library staff to input local information on to a microcomputer for subsequent automated searching of the OCLC database.

Descriptors: Retrospective conversion

MICRODISCLOSURE

Supplier: Disclosure
5161 River Road, Bethesda, MD 20816, USA
Tel: 800 638 8076

Operating System: PC DOS

Hardware: IBM PC; IBM PC XT

Notes: Searches Disclosure online database. Downloads and stores data, searches the downloaded file and tabulates results.

Descriptors: Online access to Disclosure

MICROFILE

Supplier: Heyden Datasystems
Spectrum House, Hillview Gardens, London, NW4 2JQ, UK
Tel: 01 203 5171

Hardware: Apple II Plus; Apple IIe

Requirements: Apple II Plus 48K RAM, Apple IIe dual disk drives

Price: 54 pounds sterling plus 2.50 pounds sterling p & p

Notes: Will manage libraries of assorted publications, collections of music, stamps, coins etc. Each record may be identified with up to 80 keywords.

Descriptors: Catalogues; information retrieval

MICROINDEX

Supplier: Farestead Associates
24 Astley Road, Hemel Hempstead, Herts, HP1 1AA, UK
Tel: 0442 51708

Hardware: Apple II; Commodore pet 8000 series

Price: 80 pounds sterling

Notes: Specifically designed for book indexing but has a wide range of other applications

Descriptors: Book indexes; indexes

MICROLIBRARY

Supplier: Sydney Development Corp
1385 West 8th Avenue, Vancouver, BC, V6H 3V9, Canada
Tel: 604 734 8822

Notes: See other entry

MICROLIBRARY

Supplier: Sydney Dataproducts Inc
11075 Santa Monica Blvd, Suite 100, Los Angeles, CA 90025, USA
Tel: 800 992 9778

Notes: See other entry

MICROLIBRARY

Supplier: Sydney Library Products
SPS House, 40 Broadgate, Beeston, Nottingham, NG9 2FW, UK
Tel: 0602 222227; tlx: 58775

Operating System: PC DOS 2.0+; MS DOS 2.0+

Hardware: IBM PC XT; IBM PC AT; IBM PC compatibles

Requirements: 256K RAM, one 5.25" floppy disk and one hard disk. Tape streamer backup is recommended

Price: From 4,500 pounds sterling

Notes: A library and information management system with modules for cataloguing and enquiry, acquisitions, circulation, serials management and MARC record interface. A database may be created to be accessed by all modules of the system. Retrospective conversion may be by converting existing machine-readable records, retrieving MARC formatted records or re-keying. The module offers authority control and will print catalogues and labels. Acquisitions includes: online supplier file; currency conversion, fund accounting; normal, temporary and standing orders. Titles under consideration may be checked with the integrated catalogue. The issue system caters for a barcode reader, reservations, overdues, borrower traps and management reports. The serials module maintains a subscription file, and enables journal check-in, claims, invoice processing and report generation. Online links to serials subscription agencies are under development. The LCMARC database on CD-ROM may be used with the catalogue module. MICROLIBRARY can be single-user or networked.

Review: The Easy Integrated Library System makes its UK debut. VINE 47 pp33-36; Micro Library - An integrated System for small to medium sized libraries. VINE 59 July 1985 pp26-34; Microlibrary, Library Micromation News, 9th Aug 1985, pp8-11

Descriptors: Acquisitions; catalogues; catalogues: online; issue system; retrospective conversion; serials control

MICROLINX CHECK-IN

Supplier: Faxon Europe
Nieuwezijds Voorburgwal 60, 1012 SC Amsterdam
Tel: 020 240885

Notes: see other entry

MICROLINX CHECK-IN

Supplier: Faxon
15 Southwest Park, Westwood, MA 02090, USA
Tel: 1 800 225 6055

Operating System: PC DOS

Hardware: IBM PC

Price: 6,000 US dollars approx

Notes: MICROLINX is a serials control system. The user may choose the form of entry for each title: either the Faxon or MARC formats or his own specification. Barcode check-in is available. The check-in procedure may be customised for the user, and single and multiple copy subscriptions can be accommodated. MICROLINX users have access to Faxon's datalinx database, Infoserv's databases and Linx courier, the electronic mail service for online, and claiming services to Faxon.

Listings of claims, new items, invoice records, library holdings and bibliographic data may be produced, and reports and claims generated. Other features include: the maintenance of routing information; binding control and the storage of financial data such as subscription, vendor and fund information. Future enhancements to the system include more sophisticated, separately priced routing, binding and fund accounting modules.
Descriptors: Circulation: serials; serials control

MICROMARC
Supplier: Library Systems and Services Inc
1395 Piccard Drive, Suite 100, Rockville, MD 20850, USA
Tel: 800 638 8725
Hardware: Apple; Columbia MPC; IBM PC
Notes: A catalogue card production system using data from MARC files. Offline, the operator keys in an LCCN, ISBN or author title search code to a file on disk. At night, LSSI polls each user's micro and reads the search keys which are run against MARC and GPO databases. When matched, a file of bibliographic records is transmitted to the user's micro. These records may be reviewed the next morning and printed on cards with spine labels, book pockets and cards as well as to 9 track tape for later use, if required
Descriptors: Catalogue cards; labels; retrospective conversion

MICROPSI
Supplier: College of Librarianship Wales, FAO Mr. R.F. Guy
Llabadarn Fawr, Aberystwyth, Dyfed, SY23 3AS, UK
Tel: (0970) 3181; tlx: 35391 (clw g)
Operating System: CP M
Notes: KWAC and NEPHIS indexing
Descriptors: Indexes

MIKRO POLYDOC
Supplier: Norsk Senter for Informatikk A S: Norwegian Centre for Informatics
Forskningsvelen 1, Postboks 350, Blindern, Oslo 3, Norway
Tel: (02) 452010
Operating System: CP M; CP M-86; MP M; MS DOS; MP M-86
Requirements: Z80, Intel 8080 or 8086 micro processor
Price: 2000 to 15000 Norwegian Kroner
Notes: Information storage and retrieval system which allows a maximum of 5 databases per system, and a maximum of 32,768 records or 8,300,000 characters per file. There are no limits to the number of characters per record. Each record may be divided into 20 different fields. The user can define field names and abbreviations, and define which fields in the database are to be field, subfield, full text or free text searchable. A generator may be used to produce indexes from the entire database or from parts of it. KWAC indexes are produced from fields or subfields, and KWOC indexes of words in a text. The layout of the indexes is designed by the user.
Descriptors: Catalogues; databases: inhouse; indexes; information retrieval

MIKROTEL
Supplier: IRS Dialtech
Department of Trade and Industry, Room 392, Ashdown House, 123 Victoria Street, London SW1E 6RB, UK
Tel: 01 212 5638 or 8225
Operating System: PC DOS 2.0+; MS DOS 2.1+
Hardware: IBM PC; IBM PC XT
Requirements: Asynchronous communications adaptor; 128K RAM
Price: 59.25 pounds sterling
Notes: Allows the user to communicate with any host computer. When connected to ESA IRS, private files may be created offline and uploaded to the main computer. Data may be downloaded in format X and data files created and interrogated. The IRS computer may be interrogated at up to 2400 baud.
Descriptors: Online search aid; online access to ESA IRS Dialtech

MIPS
Supplier: Data Retrieval Corporation of America
8989 North Deerwood, PO Box 23437, Milwaukie, WI 53223-0437, USA
Tel: 414 355 5900
Operating System: I RMX 86
Hardware: Intel ITPS 86 445
Requirements: 1000K RAM to 2000K RAM. Disk drives 35 Mb (1 unit) to 84(4 units). Tapedrive terminals 1 to 15. Maximum of 5 printers. Photocomposer APS4 Merganthaler 505.
Price: 100,000 US dollars plus. 115,000 US dollars is the minimum price for the system sold with hardware.
Notes: A Management Information Processing System designed to meet the needs of the legal community. There are 4 subsystems. The Applications Builder allows the user to address specific problems with tailored solutions. Information Processing is a sophisticated text editor enabling the drafting, revision and printing of legal documents. Information researching allows the user to search databases of legal documents, and a Photocomposition system automatically creates camera ready copy directly from databases.
Descriptors: Information retrieval; legal documents; word processing

MIRABILIS
Supplier: Central Information Service, University of London
Senate House, University of London, Malet Street, London WC1 7HU, UK
Tel: 01 636 8000 x 5089
Operating System: CP M; MS DOS; PC DOS
Hardware: Apricot; Cifer; Rair (ICL); Sirius: Superbrain; IBM PC; IBM PC AT; IBM PC XT
Price: 250 pounds sterling
Notes: General purpose free text retrieval system. MIRABILIS is a modular system. The first module, MIRMAKE, is used for setting up a new database according to the user's own specifications for record format. Records may be entered using the MIRTEXT module either from the keyboard or from an existing

compatible MIRABILIS file already stored on disk. The MIRDEX Module provides facilities for the creation and updating of inverted indexes to words and word combinations, MIRSCH allows interactive searching on indexing terms and combinations of terms. Results of a search may be saved and automatically transferred to a new MIRABILIS file by using the MIRSAVE module. MIRPOP permits the user to print records according to a user defined format. The sorting and listing of files are possible. MIRABILIS compatible software includes: CATALOGUE CARDS AND CURRENT TITLES SYSTEM.
Descriptors: Databases: inhouse; information retrieval

MITE

Supplier: Mycroft Labs Inc
2615 N Monroe Street, Tallahasse, FL 32303, USA
Tel: 904 385 1141 (sales) or 904 386 4051 (service)
Operating System: CP M; MS DOS
Hardware: Apple Macintosh
Requirements: MITE will run on CP/M or MS DOS microcomputer with minimum 128K RAM for 16 bit and 64K RAM for 8 bit micros
Price: 150 US dollars (CP/M + MS DOS); 145 US dollars (Macintosh)
Notes: Menu driven multi protocol asynchronous communications package with auto dialing, auto answer and auto logon. Permits the downloading of binary and text files. Enables the micro to access asynchronous ASCII online systems, e.g. The Source, Newsnet, Dow Jones, and also to transfer any file to another micro. MITE PLUS is an enhanced version of MITE and permits the emulation of terminals such as the VT100, Televideo 950 and IBM 3101
Descriptors: Communications; online search aid

MITINET RETRO

Supplier: Information Transform Inc, FAO Hank Epstein
502 Leonard Street, Madison, WI 53711, USA
Operating System: DOS 3.3; PC DOS 2.1+
Hardware: Apple II Plus; Apple IIe; IBM PC
Requirements: Apple IIe 48K RAM, IBM PC 128K RAM
Price: 250 US dollars software. 140 US dollars comfiche catalogue of 1,500,000 LC MARC titles for matching
Notes: Retrospective catalogue conversion on an Apple or IBM PC. Interface to COM catalogue vendor to obtain MARC tapes and COM catalogues and CD-ROM catalogues.
Review: Information Technology and Libraries 2 (2) (June 1983) pp166-173; School Library Journal (March 1985) pp109-112
Descriptors: Catalogues; retrospective conversion

N I C SEARCH PACKAGE

Supplier: Stichting N.I.C., FAO Hans van Nieuwkerk
PO Box 36, 2600 AA Delft, The Netherlands
Tel: 31 15569330; tlx: 38071 zptno
Hardware: TRS 100 portable
Price: 1000 US dollars including hardware
Notes: Features include automatic logon, offline preparation of searches, tape storage of SDI's and downloaded files and session cost calculation during terminal use.
Descriptors: Online search aid

NEWSDEX

Supplier: Capital Systems Group Inc
11301 Rockville Pike, Kensington, MD 20895, USA
Tel: (301)881-9400
Operating System: TRS DOS; PC DOS
Hardware: IBM PC; IBM PC XT; TRS 80 model II
Requirements: Printer
Price: 450 US dollars
Notes: Prepares and cumulates newspaper indexes. Data entry to the system is prompted, and entries can be reviewed and edited on screen. Subject headings may be produced, and authority control is available. Entries may be sorted and formatted before the printed index is produced.
Descriptors: Indexes

NONESUCH ACQUISITIONS SYSTEM

Supplier: Ringgold Management Systems
Box 368, Beaverton, Oregon 97075-0368, USA
Tel: (503) 645 3502
Hardware: IBM PC; IBM PC compatibles; Wang PC
Requirements: Wang PC needs Basic 2
Price: 2,500 US dollars per terminal to a maximum of 15,000 US dollars. Special quotations will be made for multiple systems.
Notes: Online acquisitions control system featuring: pre-acquisitions searching; order preparation; open order maintenance; vendor reports; receiving and invoice processing; automatic fund accounting; enquiry by vendor, requestor and title. Offline operations are: automatic claiming; automatic cancellations; in-process control; accessions lists; vendor performance analysis and management reports.
Descriptors: Acquisitions

NONESUCH CIRCULATION SYSTEM

Supplier: Ringgold Management Systems
Box 368, Beaverton, Oregon 97075, USA
Tel: (503) 645-3502
Operating System: CP M; MP M; MS DOS; PC DOS; TRS DOS; UNIX; XENIX
Hardware: IBM PC; IBM PC compatibles; Wang PC
Requirements: Software will run on other microcomputers with Cobol
Price: 2,500 US dollars per terminal up to 15,000 US dollars. Special quotations made for multiple systems
Notes: Uses one or more circulation systems linked to a large disk store. Stations consist of a microcomputer screen and keyboard, barcode reader and floppy disk drive. The small test system handles up to 50,000 records (items and borrowers) Online features include: charge; discharge; renewal; patron holds; item reserves; enquiry by patron or item author or title; patron registration and fines. Offline features are: overdues; end of term notices; special lists; physical inventory and statistical summaries.

Descriptors: Issue system

NOTA BENE

Supplier: Anne Yates, Oxford University Press
Walton Street, Oxford, OX2 6DP, UK
Tel: 0865-56767; tlx: 837330 oxpress;
telefax: 0865 56646
Notes: See other entry

NOTA BENE

Supplier: "Hands-on" Microcomputer Learning Centre
55 North Street, Brighton, BN1 1RH, UK
Tel: 0273 736081
Operating System: PC DOS 2.0+
Hardware: IBM PC; IBM PC compatibles
Requirements: 256K RAM, two double sided floppy disk drives or hard disk
Notes: NOTA BENE combines features of a multi-lingual word processor with those of a "text-base" system. The user may choose from five major styles of organisation, a multi level table of contents in a variety of formats may be produced, and notes are automatically numbered and renumbered. The program generates a bibliography from titles marked in the document and can generate up to three multi-level indexes. A "text-base" of quotations, comments, reviews or any relevant information may be created. Every word in the "text-base" is indexed and can be searched upon, viewed and inserted into a document, if required. The system caters for most major western European languages, and a special version, using a different video display card, will allow the display and printing of additional alphabets with selected printers. Tables and charts may also be created. Additional features include: split and full-screen windows; mailmerge, and program customisation.
Descriptors: Bibliographies; indexes; information retrieval; word processing

NUTSHELL INFORMATION FILER 2.0

Supplier: Leading Edge Software Products
21 Highland Circle, Needham Heights, MA 02194, USA
Tel: (617) 449-4655; (800) 343-3436
Operating System: PC DOS 2.0+; MS DOS 2.0+
Hardware: IBM PC; IBM PC XT; IBM PC AT; IBM PC compatibles
Requirements: 256K RAM; IBM PC compatibles must be 100
Price: 150 US dollars, including manual and tutorial
Notes: NUTSHELL is a menu-driven database manager offering virtually unlimited field and record size, automatic indexing, data validation, ditto and undo features. User-defined screen display permits multiple layouts for viewing and generating reports. NUTSHELL also offers mailing label support up to 9-across, input and output to ASCII, DIF, dBase and other formats. Tutorial and sample files included. Technical specifications max 60,000 fields per record, max 16 milliom characters per field, max 16 million characters per record, subject to hardware limitations. Query speed: a single item search locates a unique record from 1000 seconds in two records. All fields are keys.
Review: Project database, PC Magazine, July 1986
Descriptors: Information retrieval

OCELOT ACQUISITIONS MODULE

Supplier: Tescor Inc
461 Carlisle Drive, Hemdon, VI 22070, USA
Tel: 010 1 703 435 9501
Notes: See other entry

OCELOT ACQUISITIONS MODULE

Supplier: ACI Computer Services
310 Fern Tree Gully Road, North Clayton, Victoria, Australia 3168
Tel: 010 61 3 544 8433
Notes: See other entry

OCELOT ACQUISITIONS MODULE

Supplier: Oriel Computers
Prins Hendrikkade 22, 1012 TM Amsterdam, The Netherlands
Tel: 020 258499
Notes: See other entry

OCELOT ACQUISITIONS MODULE

Supplier: Oriel Computer Services Ltd
1-5 West Street, Chipping Norton, Oxfordshire OX7 5LY, UK
Tel: 0608 41351; tlx: 837512 oriel g
Price: 1995 pounds sterling
Notes: See other entry

OCELOT ACQUISITIONS MODULE

Supplier: Aball Software Inc
2268 Osler Street, Regina, Saskatchewan, Canada, S4P 1W8
Tel: (010-1-306)569-2180
Operating System: PC DOS 2.X; PC DOS 3.X
Hardware: IBM PC; IBM PC XT; IBM PC AT; IBM PC compatibles
Requirements: 256K RAM 80 column printer, hard disk and floppy disk drive
Notes: Supports order requests, orders, claims and cancellations. Multiple copies, multi location and multi fund orders can be accommodated, and serials may be ordered with one issue/detail. The system permits report generation and fund accounting, and a vendor sub module maintains vendor records. Year-end processor re-sets files for new budget year. Security is provided through passwords and security levels assigned to operators.
Review: Bazillion, R.J. and Scott, S. Ocelot unleashed. Canadian Library Journal, 42 (3) 1985, pp155-158.
Descriptors: Acquisitions

OCELOT CATALOGUE MODULE

Supplier: Tescor Inc
461 Carlisle Drive, Hemdon, VI 22070, USA
Tel: 010 1 703 435 9501
Notes: See other entry

OCELOT CATALOGUE MODULE

Supplier: ACI Computer Services
310 Fern Tree Gully Road, North Clayton,
Victoria, Australia 3168
Tel: 010 61 3 544 8433
Notes: See other entry

OCELOT CATALOGUE MODULE

Supplier: Oriel Computers
Prins Hendrikkade 22, 1012 TM Amsterdam,
The Netherlands
Tel: 020 258499
Notes: See other entry

OCELOT CATALOGUE MODULE

Supplier: Oriel Computer Services Ltd
1-5 West Street, Chipping Norton,
Oxfordshire, OX7 5LY, UK
Tel: 0608-41351; tlx: 837512 oriel g
Notes: See other entry

OCELOT CATALOGUE MODULE

Supplier: Aball Software Inc
2268 Osler Street, Regina, Saskatchewan,
Canada, S4P 1W8
Operating System: MS DOS 2.x; MS DOS 3.x; PC DOS 2.x; PC DOS 3.x
Hardware: IBM PC; IBM PC XT; IBM PC AT; IBM PC compatibles
Requirements: 256K RAM, 80 column printer, hard disk and floppy disk drive
Price: 1995 pounds sterling
Notes: Supports MARC compatible bibliographic records. Each citation can have 8 names, subjects and titles, in addition to imprint, date, class number, ISBN, ISSN, BNB number, 1900 character notes, etc. Copy, edit and delete functions are available together with spine label and card set printing. The system provides author, subject and title searches, keywords and Boolean logic, with numeric and bibliography searches as additional possibilities. Authority control is provided for all names, subjects and titles entered as part of a catalogue record. Enquirers are automatically routed to preferred terms. MARC interface available for downloading.
Review: Bazillion, R.J. and Scott, S. Ocelot unleashed. Canadian Library Journal, 42 (3) 1985, pp155-158
Descriptors: Catalogues; catalogues: online; MARC interface

OCELOT CIRCULATION MODULE

Supplier: Tescor Inc
461 Carlisle Drive, Hemdon, VI 22070, USA
Tel: 010 1 703 435 9501
Notes: See other entry

OCELOT CIRCULATION MODULE

Supplier: ACI Computer Services
310 Fern Tree Gully Road, North Clayton,
Victoria, Australia 3168
Tel: 010 61 3 544 8433
Notes: See other entry

OCELOT CIRCULATION MODULE

Supplier: Oriel Computers
Prins Hendrikkade 22, 1012 TM Amsterdam,
The Netherlands
Tel: 020 258499
Notes: See other entry

OCELOT CIRCULATION MODULE

Supplier: Oriel Computer Services Ltd
1-5 West Street, Chipping Norton,
Oxfordshire, OX7 5LY, UK
Tel: 0608 41351; tlx: 837512 oriel g
Price: 995 pounds sterling
Notes: See other entry

OCELOT CIRCULATION MODULE

Supplier: Aball Software Inc
2268 Osler Street, Regina, Saskatchewan,
Canada, S4P 1W8
Operating System: PC DOS 2.X; PC DOS 3.X
Hardware: IBM PC; IBM PC XT; IBM PC AT; IBM PC compatibles
Requirements: 256K RAM, 80 column printer, 10 Mb hard disk and floppy disk drive. Barcode reader optional.
Notes: Supports check in, check out, fines, reservations, status reports for items and borrowers, traps, statistical reports. Access to individual functions under password control. Catalogue interface is provided by wanding barcodes into the CATALOGUE module. Circulation records are automatically generated from the catalogue record without re-keying. Author, title, call number, subject searching available.
Review: Bazillion, R.J. and Scott, S. Ocelot unleashed. Canadian Library Journal, 42 (3) 1985, pp155-158
Descriptors: Issue system

OCELOT LIBRARY SYSTEM

Supplier: Tescor Inc
461 Carlisle Drive, Hemdon, VI 22070, USA
Tel: 010 1 703 435 9501
Notes: See other entry

OCELOT LIBRARY SYSTEM

Supplier: ACI Computer Services
310 Fern Tree Gully Road, North Clayton,
Victoria, Australia 3168
Tel: 010 61 3 544 8433
Notes: See other entry

OCELOT LIBRARY SYSTEM

Supplier: Oriel Computers
Prins Hendrikkade 22, 1012 TM Amsterdam,
The Netherlands
Tel: 020 258499
Notes: See other entry

OCELOT LIBRARY SYSTEM

Supplier: Oriel Computer Services Ltd
1-5 West Street, Chipping Norton,
Oxfordshire, OX7 5LY, UK
Tel: 0608 41351; tlx: 837512 oriel g
Notes: See other entry

OCELOT LIBRARY SYSTEM

Supplier: Aball Software Inc
2268 Osler Street, Regina, Saskatchewan,
Canada, S4P 1W8
Operating System: PC DOS 2.X; PC DOS 3.X
Hardware: IBM PC; IBM PC XT; IBM PC AT; IBM PC compatibles
Price: No price available
Notes: A suite of modules that interact to produce an integral library system. Modules can be purchased separately and integrated retroactively. Consists of acquisitions, catalogues, circulation and serials, described in detail under these headings. See OCELOT ACQUISITIONS, CATALOGUE, CIRCULATION and SERIALS modules.
Review: Bazillion, R.J. and Scott, S. Ocelot unleashed. Canadian Library Journal, 42 (3) 1985, pp155-158
Descriptors: Acquisitions; catalogues: online; issue system; serials control

OCELOT SERIALS MODULE

Supplier: Tescor Inc
461 Carlisle Drive, Hemdon, VI 22070, USA
Tel: 010 1 703 435 9501
Notes: See other entry

OCELOT SERIALS MODULE

Supplier: ACI Computer Services
310 Fern Tree Gully Road, North Clayton,
Victoria, Australia 3168
Tel: 010 61 3 544 8433
Notes: See other entry

OCELOT SERIALS MODULE

Supplier: Oriel Computers
Prins Hendrikkade 22, 1012 TM Amsterdam,
The Netherlands
Tel: 020 258499
Notes: See other entry

OCELOT SERIALS MODULE

Supplier: Oriel Computer Services Ltd
1-5 West Street, Chipping Norton,
Oxfordshire, OX7 5LY, UK
Tel: 0608 41351; tlx: 837512 oriel g
Notes: See other entry

OCELOT SERIALS MODULE

Supplier: Aball Software Inc
2268 Osler St, Regina, Saskatchewan,
Canada, S4P 1W8
Tel: (010-1-306)569-2180
Operating System: MS DOS 2.X; MS DOS 5.X
Hardware: IBM PC; IBM PC XT; IBM PC AT; IBM PC compatibles
Requirements: 256K RAM, 80 column printer, hard disk and one floppy disk drive
Notes: A full service serials control program. Calendar based, automatic receipt prediction, route lists, bindery, claims, order and renew. Fund accounting and vendor file similar to OCELOT ACQUISITIONS MODULE. Interfaces to Catalogue and Circulation Modules. Stand alone version has Title and Subject keyword searching as well as volume, date, ISSN, call number, etc.
Review: Bazillion, R.J. and Scott, S. Ocelot unleashed. Canadian Library Journal, 42 (3) 1985, pp155-158
Descriptors: Serials control

OCLC ILL MICRO ENHANCER

Supplier: OCLC Europe
2nd Floor, Lloyds Bank Chambers, 75
Edmund Street, Birmingham, B3 3HA, UK
Tel: 021 236 3224; tlx: 335176 oclc tfstrs g
Operating System: Apple II
Notes: See other entry

OCLC ILL MICRO ENHANCER

Supplier: OCLC
6565 Frantz Road, Dublin, Ohio 43017, USA
Tel: (614) 764-60000
Operating System: PC DOS
Hardware: IBM PC; IBM PC XT
Requirements: 256K RAM and printer, with the following modems: Hayes smartmodem 300, 1200 or 1200b, US Robotics AD212A or Password, Multi Tech MT 12hc or MT 212AH
Price: 275 US dollars
Notes: Allows users to prepare transactions with OCLC offline on the microcomputer and specify a time when the PC will dial the OCLC computer and carry out the tasks automatically. Functions include dispatch, receipt and return of items, cancellation of requests, recalling materials, refusing pending requests, completing transactions and printing out incoming requests.
Review: Stigleman, S. ILL micro enhancer: for OCLC interlibrary loans. Electronic Library, 4 (3), June 1986, pp146-149
Descriptors: Interlibrary loans

OFFICE MANAGER

Supplier: Missing Link Computers Ltd
65 Maygrove Road, London, NW6 2EG, UK
Tel: 01 625 5111
Operating System: PC DOS; MS DOS
Hardware: Commodore; Fortune; IBM PC; Sirius
Notes: Database management system customised to form library loans system
Descriptors: Issue system

OLSAM: ONLINE SEARCH ASSISTANCE MACHINE

Supplier: Franklin Research Center
20th and Race Streets, Philadelphia, PA
19103, USA
Operating System: CP M
Hardware: North Star
Requirements: Software is delivered on North Star's UCSD Pascal format double density 5.25" floppy disks

Price: 995 US dollars. 7500 US dollars with hardware. Manual 50 US dollars

Notes: Accesses Dialog and SDC databases using a single command language

Review: Toliver, D.E. "OLSAM: an intelligent front end for bibliographic information retrieval". Information Technology and Libraries. December 1982 1(4) pp317-326

Descriptors: Online access to Dialog; online access to SDC; online search aid

ON TYME

Supplier: CLASS
1415 Koll Circle, Suite 101, San Jose, CA 95112-4698, USA
Tel: 408 289 1756

Price: No price available

Notes: An electronic mail system for libraries. The network consists of more than 700 libraries and permits local, national and international communications. Interlibrary loans are facilitated.

Descriptors: Electronic mail; interlibrary loans

ONLINE PRICING SIMULATOR

Supplier: Online Simulations Inc
PO Box 310, Harrods Creek, KY 40027, USA

Operating System: CP M; PC DOS

Hardware: Apple; IBM PC; TRS

Price: 125 US dollars. Includes software, manual and registration card

Notes: Package for online pricing and modelling analyses. Eliminates most hand calculations related to online pricing and online usage cost estimates. The program is menu driven and offers 4 specific applications. First, the cost of a search in a bibliographic database may be estimated before going online. Second, it is possible to project publisher royalties or item sharing vendor revenues per database. Third, file specific changes may be analysed over a period of 1 to 24 months using up to 5 variables. Finally, a table of 24 representative databases' royalty rates and vendor prices may be considered.

Descriptors: Finances; online search aid; statistics

OPAC ACCESS

Supplier: Leicester Polytechnic Library
PO Box 143, Leicester, LE1 9BH, UK
Tel: 0533 551551

Hardware: Olivetti M24

Requirements: Also runs on M24 compatibles running G.W. Basic

Price: Depends on number ordered

Notes: Allows access to a page organised on-line public access catalogue, in house. Enables storing of references editing and printing, developed for the use with BLCMP OPAC. Runs at 300 baud.

Descriptors: Catalogues: online

ORCHARD SYSTEMS CIRCULATION MANAGEMENT SYSTEM

Supplier: Orchard Systems
207 East Third Street, Waunakee, WI 53597, USA
Tel: (608)849-5727

Operating System: DOS 3.3

Hardware: APPLE II

Requirements: 48K RAM and Applesoft, single disk drive and 132 column printer

Price: 125 US dollars

Notes: Tracks up to 600 items on loan

Descriptors: Issue system

ORDERIT

Supplier: Right On Programs
PO Box 977, Huntingdon, NY 11743, USA

Hardware: Apple II Plus; Apple IIe; Commodore pet; Commodore 64; IBM PC; TRS 80

Requirements: Minimum 32K RAM

Price: 40 US dollars

Notes: The system prompts the user to input order information which may then be printed. Items are deleted from the program when they arrive.

Descriptors: Acquisitions

ORICAT

Supplier: Elhanan Adler
University of Haifa Library, Haifa 31999, Israel

Operating System: CP M; MS DOS

Hardware: IBM PC; Superbrain

Price: On application

Notes: A cataloguing program which permits entry in Hebrew

Descriptors: Catalogues

OVERDUE BOOKS

Supplier: Right On Programs
PO Box 977, Huntingdon, NY 11743, USA

Hardware: Apple II Plus; Apple IIe; Commodore pet; Commodore 64; IBM PC; TRS 80

Requirements: Minimum 32K RAM

Price: 50 US dollars

Notes: Intended for school libraries. Information about outstanding books may be recalled on the screen or on the printer, enabling listings to be produced

Descriptors: Overdues; school libraries

OVERDUE COLLECTOR

Supplier: Follett Software Company
4506 Northwest Highway, Crystal Lake, IL 60014, USA
Tel: (800) 435-6170; (815) 455-1100

Hardware: Apple II plus; TRS 80 model III

Requirements: 48K RAM and 80 column printer

Price: 49.95 US dollars

Notes: Automtically transfers week after week all the active records from the individual OVERDUE WRITER disks so that one cumulative disk of all the "bad guys" can be maintained.

Descriptors: Overdues

OVERDUE WRITER

Supplier: Follett Software Company
4506 Northwest Highway, Crystal Lake, IL 60014, USA
Tel: (800) 435-6170; (815)455-1100
Hardware: Apple II plus; TRS 80 model III
Requirements: 48K RAM and 80 column printer
Notes: Specifically designed for small libraries, it will keep track of check-outs, search all records and print lists, overdues and bills
Descriptors: Issue system

OVERNIGHT WRITER

Supplier: Follett Software Company
4506 Northwest Highway, Crystal Lake, IL 60014, USA
Tel: (800)435-6170; (815)455-1100e
Hardware: Apple II plus; TRS 80 model III
Requirements: 48K RAM and 80 column printer
Price: 49.95 US dollars
Notes: Abridged version of OVERDUE WRITER for short term loans. Designed to handle the specific problems of overnight and short term checkouts. Information on up to 150 items can be entered at the end of the day or early the next day after the materials have become overdue.
Descriptors: Issue system

PC ABSTRACTS ACCESS PAK

Supplier: FYI Inc
4202 Spicewood Springs Road, Suite 204, Austin, Texas 78759, USA
Operating System: PCDOS
Hardware: IBM PC; IBM PC compatibles
Price: 149 US dollars annual subscription
Notes: PC ABSTRACTS are citations and summaries for every article in 10 PC journals including Byte, Softalk, PC Magazine, PC World and PC Tech Journal, since 1983. It is possible to search on every word or number in a file. There is a Graphic Program Interface, Data Encryption protection and diskette finger print copy protection. Abstracts may be searched, retrieved, displayed on the screen and printed, with several print options available. Each ACCESS PAK can handle up to 65,000 entries in each file, with up to 300K of free style ASCII characters in each entry.
Descriptors: Information retrieval: commercial database subsets

PC DIAL

Supplier: Personal Bibliographic Software Inc
PO Box 4250, Ann Arbor, MI 48106, USA
Tel: 313 996 1580
Operating System: PC DOS
Hardware: IBM PC; IBM PC XT
Price: 25 US dollars
Notes: A communications program that provides for the recording of the conversation between the mainframe and the microcomputer in a standard DOS disk file. Developed for use with BIBLIO LINK and the PROFESSIONAL BIBLIOGRAPHIC SYSTEM
Descriptors: Communications; online search aid

PC NET LINK

Supplier: Informatics General Corporation
Library Services Division, 6011 Executive Boulevard, Rockville, MD 20852, USA
Tel: (800)638-6595
Operating System: PC DOS
Hardware: IBM PC XT; IBM PC AT
Requirements: Hard disk, printer and Hayes smartmodem 1200 or Genazyz Telios telecommunications software
Price: 550 US dollars
Notes: Reduces online time and costs when accessing and searching multiple databases, and simplifies the selection of databases from a variety of hosts by using menu driven selection or name. Automatic connect, disconnect, logging on and off to individual files is supported.
Descriptors: Online search aid

PEARL 4.0

Supplier: CLSI Ltd (UK)
Regent Arcade House, 252-260 Regent Street, London W1R 5DA, UK
Tel: 01 4378090
Notes: See other entry

PEARL 4.0

Supplier: CLSI Inc
1220 Washington Street, West Newton, MA 02165, USA
Tel: 617 965 6310
Notes: See other entry

PEARL 4.0

Supplier: Blackwell Library Systems Inc
202 East Main Street, Suite 105, Huntingdon, NY 11743, USA
Tel: 516 351 1611 or 800 645 5395
Notes: See other entry

PEARL 4.0

Supplier: Blackwell Technical Services Ltd
North Hinksey Lane, Botley, Oxford, OX2 OLX, UK
Tel: 0865 731751
Operating System: MUMPS
Hardware: DEC professional
Notes: PEARL supports the ordering of books and serials by automating check in, claiming, fund accounting, binding, loan control and circulation, online public access catalogues and management reporting. A compatible word processing package is available if required. Issue information can be manipulated to form the basis of a current awareness service. Full MARC format input and output are currently under development.
Descriptors: Acquisitions; bibliographies; catalogues; catalogues: online; circulation: serials; issue system; orders: online; serials control

PERCS

Supplier: Central Information Service, University of London
University of London, Senate House, Malet Street, London WC1E 7HU, UK
Tel: 01 636 8000 x5089
Operating System: MS DOS; PC DOS
Hardware: Apricot; IBM PC; IBM PC AT; IBM PC XT; IBM PC compatibles; Sirius; Apricot
Price: 750 pounds sterling
Notes: PERCS is a periodicals control system designed to maintain databases storing details of periodicals subscribed to, periodicals as received, readers and circulation slips. The system is designed for small libraries and will manage databases storing a maximum of 1400 records.
Descriptors: Serials control

PERIODICALS

Supplier: Counting House Programs C/O James Thompson
123 Green End Road, Hemel Hempstead, Herts, UK
Tel: 0442 54845
Hardware: Commodore 8000 series
Price: 100 pounds sterling
Notes: Serials control including circulation and accounting features
Descriptors: Circulation: serials; serials control

PERSONAL BIBLIOGRAPHIC SYSTEM

Supplier: Personal Bibliographic Software Inc
PO Box 4250, Ann Arbor, MI 48106, USA
Tel: (313) 996-1580
Hardware: Apple II; Apple II plus; Apple IIe; Apple IIc; Apple III
Requirements: One 5.25" disk drive
Price: 195 US Dollars; demo disk 75 US dollars
Notes: The personal bibliographic system is a specialized text-formatting system that enables users to create and maintain formatted bibliographies. Features include: variable-length fields and records, searching with Boolean logic on all fields, and a full-screen editor. Formats bibliographies according to the ANSI standard using 20 different document types, including books, journal articles, maps, letters, manuscripts, reports, and new papers.
Review: Library Software Review - June 1984; Educational Technology - July 1984; Technicalities - Jan. 1984
Descriptors: Bibliographies; information retrieval; word processing

PET COMPUTER LIBRARY CARD MAKER

Supplier: John Horemans
2588 Inlake Ct., Mississauga, Ontario, Canada L5N 2A7
Hardware: Commodore pet
Requirements: Minimum 16K RAM, Basic 4.0, C2N datasette or 4040 disk drive, I.D.S. 440 printer paper tiger
Price: 100 US dollars for tape. 110 US dollars for disk
Notes: Prints up to 7 cards from one input
Descriptors: Catalogue cards

PINDOC

Supplier: Pinpoint Analysis Ltd
Mercury House, 117 Waterloo Road, London SE1 8UL, UK
Tel: 01-928-1874
Operating System: MS DOS; PC DOS
Hardware: Bull micral 30; IBM PC XT; IBM PC AT; IBM PC compatibles; Olivetti M24; Logabax personna 1600; Thompson Micromega 160; Victor
Price: No price available
Notes: PINDOC is an information storage and retrieval system which provides three types of file for the user: the catalogue where the file definition records are stored; document files; and indexes which are created from fields. Several fields can be inverted into a single index and one file may be linked to several indexes. The default limits on the system may be modified.if necessary, but they are set to 4,000 characters and 99 fields per document with 10 indexes per file. The file definition may be modified at any time, and global corrections of documents are possible. Query mode permits Boolean searching, range searching, right, left and internal truncation and the manipulation of previously generated sets. Files may be chained together for more effective organisation of data, subfiles may be created or files may be fully or partially merged. Sort keys can be taken from one or several fields and sophisticated output formats are possible. A programming language is integrated into the package to allow front-end menus or data input prompts to be set up. This facility is fully incorporated into PINDOC but forms a separate package if the software is purchased as TEXTO from vendors outside the UK.
Descriptors: Databases: inhouse; information retrieval

PLIDOS

Supplier: Fachinformationszentrum Technik e.V.
Ostbahnhofstr 13, Frankfurt, 1 D 6000, W Germany
Tel: 049 611 4308 225; tlx: 4 189 459 fizt d
Operating System: Commodore DOS
Hardware: Commodore 8032; Commodore 8050
Requirements: Minimum 32K RAM, 2x1/2 Mb disk drives, acoustic coupler with interface adapter, basic compiler
Price: Up to 5000 US dollars
Notes: The Persoenliches Literatur Informations und Dokumentations System is an information system which allows entry, storage and retrieval of information. It also permits access to online databases via several telecommunication networks. Conversion of stored citations from external databases into the format of a local information system is possible. The system offers Boolean searching and truncation as well as SDI and print functions.
Descriptors: Information retrieval; online search aid; reference management

POPPYTIME INDEX BUILD SYSTEM

Supplier: Poppytime Ltd
40 Triton Square, London, NW1 3HG, UK
Tel: 01 387 4599
Hardware: IBM PC; Sirius; Xerox 820

Price: 5500 pounds sterling plus VAT including hardware. 950 pounds sterling plus VAT software only
Notes: The package is used to create indexes. Index items are entered using a simple data entry screen. Word processor editing functions are available within each field. A function key enables any or all fields to be copied from an existing index item. Items may be recalled at any time for inspection or amendment. Listings can be printed in any sequence. The word processing facilities may also be used for correspondence and reports. The capacity of the system is dependent on the disks used.
Descriptors: Indexes; word processing

POPPYTIME INFORMATION RETRIEVAL SYSTEM

Supplier: Poppytime Ltd
40 Triton Square, London, NW1 3HG, UK
Tel: 01 387 4599
Hardware: Commodore 8032
Requirements: 8050 disk drive
Price: 2700 pounds sterling plus VAT including hardware, 300 pounds sterling plus VAT software only
Notes: Handles technical abstracts and similar data. The main text or "title" of each record may be up to 250 characters long. The record, including keywords and authors, may contain up to 1000 characters. Keywords may be generated automatically from the "title", and other keywords may be entered separately. The system prints a sorted report of all keywords in use which can be used to correct errors and to provide a lexicon for manual control of new input. Records may be transferred between disks. Each floppy disk can hold approximately 700 records of 1000 characters each. The software may also be used for word processing purposes.
Descriptors: Databases: inhouse; information retrieval; word processing

POST PLUS

Supplier: Mctel
Three Bala Plaza East, Suite 505, Bala, Cynwyd, PA 19004, USA
Tel: 215 668 0983
Operating System: CP M; MS DOS; TRS DOS
Notes: Integrates telecommunications and word processing. Messages may be prepared using a full screen editor. The communications session is saved to disk for later review and editing. There are built in automatic logon sequences for more than 12 online information and electronic mail services. Permits communication with other micros.
Descriptors: Communications; online search aid; word processing

POST PLUS BRIEFCASE

Supplier: Mctel
Three Bala Plaza East, Suite 505, Bala, Cynwyd, PA 19004, USA
Tel: 215 668 0983
Hardware: Epson PX 8
Price: 249 US dollars
Notes: ROM chip available for the Epson PX 8. Incorporates all the features of POST PLUS.
Descriptors: Communications; online search aid; word processing

POST PLUS CONCURRENT

Supplier: Mctel
Three Bala Plaza East, Suite 505, Bala, Cynwyd, PA 19004, USA
Tel: 215 668 0983
Hardware: IBM PC; IBM PC compatibles
Price: 795 US dollars or 995 US dollars with optional built in modem
Notes: Incorporates all the features of POST PLUS. Carries out communications and printing tasks whilst the user carries out other tasks.
Descriptors: Communications; online search aid; word processing

PREDITOR

Supplier: Information Management Consultants Ltd
MIMAC Unit, Liverpool Polytechnic, Byrom St, Liverpool, L3 3AF, UK
Tel: 051-207-2725 or 051-207-3581 x 2028; tlx: 627993 mimac g
Hardware: BBC model B
Price: PREDITOR 95 pounds sterling; AUTO 150 pounds sterling; MASKER 15 pounds sterling; DUMPER 60 pounds sterling; RESPONDER 25 pounds sterling; RESPONDER 2 85 pounds sterling; DATABASE 65 pounds sterling
Notes: Programs to interact with viewdata and other remote databases and to edit and display viewdata frames locally. PREDITOR permits on-line and off-line viewing and editing, off-line response frame preparation, graphics and local database operation. AUTO retrieves and saves pages from a viewdatabase and automatically amends existing pages with newly edited pages. MASKER allows automatic changing or masking of stored pages. DUMPER carousels nests to either single or multiple screens, or to a printer. RESPONDER retrieves and stores pages from a remote database, and enables off-line completion of response frames and message box frames; RESPONDER 2 has automatic error correction. DATABASE turns a BBC micro into a interactive viewdatabase, accessed from the local keyboard or via modem and RS423 port. FILER converts normal files to videotex frames and prints a collection of videotex frames as a 3-column A4 newspaper.
Descriptors: Viewdata: inhouse systems; viewdata: access to remote systems

PRISM

Supplier: Prism Micro Products Ltd
Prism House, 18/19 Mora Street, City Road, London, UK
Hardware: IBM PC; BBC; Apple II; Sirius
Price: IBM 259 pounds sterling; BBC 89.95 pounds sterling; Apple 129 pounds sterling; Sirius 259 pounds sterling
Notes: Four systems available, one for each micro. Each system contains a modem, an interface cable and the relevant viewdata communications software, on ROM in the case of the BBC system, on disk for the IBM and Sirius, and on disk with a communications card for the

Apple. In addition to allowing the user to access Prestel, Micronet 800 and other viewdata services, the IBM and the Sirius systems allow reformatting of downloaded viewdata pages for further processing. Messages can be created offline and sent. Files may be transferred between IBM, Sirius and other computers.
Descriptors: Viewdata: access to remote systems

PRIVATE TUTOR

Supplier: IBM Authorised Retail Centres
see telephone directory for local address
Tel: see telephone directory for local telephone
Operating System: PC DOS
Hardware: IBM PC
Requirements: Minimum 96K RAM
Price: 42 pounds sterling
Notes: A librarian may use this to create a programmed course of instruction
Review: PC User May 1984 pp85-90
Descriptors: User Education

PRO SEARCH

Supplier: Micromedia Ltd, FAO Marcia Olmstead
158 Pearl Street, Toronto, Ontario, Canada M5H IL1
Tel: (416) 593-5211; (800) 387-2689
Notes: See other entry

PRO SEARCH

Supplier: CLASS
1415 Koll Circle, Suite 101, San Jose, CA 95112-4698, USA
Tel: (408) 289-1756
Operating System: PC DOS; MS DOS
Hardware: IBM PC; IBM PC XT; IBM PC AT; IBM PC Compatibles; Texas Instruments professional computers
Price: 495 US dollars
Notes: An online, front end search software package which supports both Dialog and BRS. An expanded version of In Search, PRO SEARCH incorporates all of the original capabilities of In Search, whilst adding new features. These include: the use of BRS commands while searching Dialog, and vice versa; full compatibility with Dialog version 2; a cost accounting feature which tracks searching costs automatically and identifies search sessions by date, time, database searched, customer name or department code and searcher name. Monthly summaries can be generated. Search strategies can be formulated and refined before a user goes online and then executed by a single keystroke. The software includes database information from Dialog's Blue Sheets and BRS' Aid Pages.
Review: Quint, Barbara. Menlo corporation's PRO SEARCH: review of a software search aid. Online 10 (1) January 1986, pp 17-25; High Technology. Jan 1986; Wilson Library Bulletin. Jan 1986; Library Hi Tech News. Feb 1986; MD Computing. July/August 1986
Descriptors: Online access to BRS; Online access to Dialog; online search aid

PRO SEARCH 1.04

Supplier: Personal Bibliographic Software Inc
PO Box 4250, Ann Arbor, MI 48106, USA
Tel: (313) 996-1580
Operating System: PC DOS 2.0+
Hardware: IBM PC; IBM PC XT; IBM PC AT; IBM PC compatibles
Requirements: 256K RAM, 320K RAM for DOS 3.0+, modem
Price: 495 US dollars, revisions 45 US dollars, major upgrades 100 US dollars, trial size disk with manual 19.95 US dollars
Notes: The PRO-SEARCH program searches BRS and Dialog using their respective command languages (with PRO-SEARCH enhancements), or using a menu-driven interface. PRO-SEARCH also searches BRS using Dialog commands, or vice versa. Reduces online connect time by enabling you to design and store your search strategies offline. Provides database-specific reference information online or off. Tracks online charges through the built-in accounting feature.
Review: Quint, Barbara. Menlo Corporation's PRO SEARCH: review of a software search aid, Online 10 (1) January 1986, pp17-25; High Technology - Jan 1986; Wilson Library Bulletin - Jan 1986; Library Hi Tech News - Feb 1986; MD Computing - July/August 1986.
Descriptors: Online access to BRS; online access to Dialog; online search aid

PRO-CITE

Supplier: Personal Bibliographic Software Inc
PO Box 4250, Ann Arbor, MI 48106, USA
Tel: (313) 996-1580
Operating System: PC DOS 2.0+
Hardware: IBM PC; IBM PC XT; IBM PC AT; IBM PC compatibles
Requirements: IBM PC compatibles must be 100
Price: 395 US dollars, upgrades 95 US dollars, sample disk 19.95 US dollars, demo 75 US dollars
Notes: PRO-CITE is a specialized database management system that enables the user to compile and maintain bibliographic information using 20 predefined and 2 user-defined document types, including books, journal articles, conference proceedings, manuscripts, and a variety of special media. Formats bibliographies according to ANSI, APA, Science Magazine or user defined standards. Index terms can be assigned to each citation for full Boolean searching. Searching, sorting, and indexing is possible on all fields. Other features include: variable-length fields and records, detection of duplicates, a full-screen editor, and context sensitive help available at all times. A PRO-CITE database can contain up to 32,500 records. With the BIBLIO-LINK companion program, the user can convert records downloaded from online databases to store and manipulate them in PRO-CITE, without having to key in these records manually. Import, a PRO-CITE utility, converts word processing text files and records from other database programs into PRO-CITE format. PRO-CITE also scans word processing documents for abbreviated, in-text bibliographic references and produces a list of the complete citations by accessing the master PRO-CITE file.
Review: Systems Librarian and Automation Review - August, 1986; Laboratory Computer Letter - Sept 1986

Descriptors: Bibliographies; information retrieval

PROFESSIONAL BIBLIOGRAPHIC SYSTEM 2.6

Supplier: Personal Bibliographic Software Inc
PO Box 4250, Ann Arbor, MI 48106, USA
Tel: 313 996 1580
Operating System: CP M
Hardware: Apple Macintosh
Requirements: 128k, single drive (dual drive recommended) runs on all macs
Price: 295 US dollars; upgrades 25 US dollars, demo disk 75 US dollars; sample disk 19.95 US dollars
Notes: The PROFESSIONAL BIBLIOGRAPHIC SYSTEM enables the user to compile and maintain bibliographic information in 20 different document types, including books, journal articles, conference proceedings, and a variety of special media. Search on all fields using Boolean operators AND, OR, and NOT combined with parentheses. Produce bibliographies according to any user-defined style sheet. ANSI, APA, MLA, and science magazine formats are predefined. Bibliographies can be transferred into Macwrite or other Macintosh word processing programs. Other features include: variable-length fields and records, a desk accessory that enables the user to change fonts, and hard disk install to run the program without a key disk. Import/export utility exchanges records with other Mac database programs.
Review: Macworld - Jan. 1986; Macuser - Feb. 1986; Small Computers in Libraries - Feb. 1986; Macazine - March 1986
Descriptors: Bibliographies; catalogues; databases: inhouse; information retrieval

PROTOKOL

Supplier: H.W. Bookservice
227 Stanley Road, Bootle, Merseyside, L20 3DY, UK
Operating System: OS 1.2
Hardware: BBC
Requirements: Disk drive and printer
Price: 26.95 pounds sterling ROM
Notes: Keeps a total record of books. Prints catalogue cards and lists, and provides search facilities. 750 records are supported on a 100K disk.
Descriptors: Accessions lists; bibliographies; catalogue cards; catalogues

PULSAR

Supplier: Litindex Inc
PO Box 2274, West Lafayette, IN 47906, USA
Hardware: TRS 80 model II
Requirements: Minimum 64K RAM and disk drive
Notes: Purdue University Literature Search and Retrieval System is a personal index system which can manage up to 20,000 references, or a file capacity of 2 Mb.
Review: Smith, F. E. et al "PULSAR: a personalized microcomputer based system for keyword search and retrieval of literature information". J. Chem. Inf. Comput. Sci. 21 (4) 1981 pp209-213
Descriptors: Reference management

PVS 990

Supplier: Mars Group Services
Shoppenhangers Road, Maidenhead, Berks, SL6 2PX, UK
Tel: 0628 39211
Operating System: DX10
Hardware: Texas Instruments DS900 range
Price: 10 year licence 3500 to 10,500 pounds sterling
Descriptors: Viewdata: access to remote systems; Viewdata: inhouse systems

QUICK SEARCH LIBRARIAN

Supplier: Interactive Microware
PO Box 771, State College, PA 16801, USA
Tel: 814 238 8294
Operating System: DOS 3.0; DOS 3.3
Hardware: Apple II
Requirements: 1 to 3 disk drives and printer
Price: 75 US dollars
Notes: A specialised file manager for capturing, sorting and searching journal literature and other serials material. Search key codes are set up by the user for accessing different subjects. Boolean searching is possible, and search strings with up to 16 elements can be used. Each produces a list which may be merged with other lists and subsequently searched using other criteria. Resulting lists may be displayed or printed by going through two menus and entering a print formatting sequence.
Review: BETTS, Francis M. "Quick search librarian. Fast but frustrating." The Electronic Library 2 (3) July 1984 pp153-155
Descriptors: Bibliographies; databases: inhouse; information retrieval

RASMUS

Supplier: Cambridge Software Ltd
PO. Box 3, Ely, Cambs, CB7 4AX, UK
Tel: 0353 4444
Operating System: CP M-86; CP M; PC DOS; MS DOS
Hardware: Apricot; IBM PC; IBM PC compatibles; Sirius
Requirements: A hard disk is recommended
Notes: The user must set up a thesaurus of keywords. Each keyword may have attached to it any number of associated keywords or subkeys. A precis must be made of all papers, bibliographies etc., and occurences of keywords underlined. The user's precis of an original document equates to an "abstract". All database records, or "abstracts" are of variable length, and there is no limit to database, record, keyword and associated keyword length. Reports may be generated. Facilities allow the sorting of selected abstracts, and the printing of letters. There is a series of communications utilities to connect to remote computers and download information.
Descriptors: Abstracts; commumnications; databases: inhouse; information retrieval; online search aid; thesaurus control

RECALL

Supplier: Insoft Ltd
35 King Street, Bristol, BS1 4DZ, UK
Tel: 0272 28893

Hardware: Act Apricot; DEC rainbow; IBM PC; IBM PC XT; IBM PC AT; IBM PC compatibles

Price: 195 pounds sterling plus VAT (as an introductory offer)

Notes: A menu driven full text retrieval system. Data are entered using conventional word processing software RECALL will accept any standard, or ASCII text file. All "significant" words are entered into a dictionary, and "common" words are excluded automatically. Boolean searching is possible. Terms containing a specified stem may be searched. Search results may be displayed, printed or written to a text file. The system may contain up to 5 "libraries" of 1000 "documents" each. A "document" may include 32000 "paragraphs" of 256 "sentences". Each "sentence" may comprise 256 words.

Descriptors: Databases: inhouse; information retrieval

REFLES: REFERENCE LIBRARIAN ENHANCEMENT SYSTEM

Supplier: University of California, Graduate School of Library and Information Science, Los Angeles and Documentation Association(DA)
Los Angeles, CA, USA

Hardware: Alpha Micro 100

Notes: For inhouse data files in a library reference department

Review: Bivins, K.T., Palmer, RC. Refles: an individual microcomputer system for fact retrieval. Online Review 4 (4) 1980, pp 357-365; Reflink: a microcomputer information retrieval system. IN: Second National Online Meeting 1981, New York, 24-26 March 1981. Learned Information, 1981, pp 73-80; Bivins, K.T., Refles (reference enhancement system): a microcomputer based database for fact retrieval and search strategy development. Paper presented at 7th Cranfield conference on Mechanised Information Storage and Retrieval Systems, July 1979; Bivins, K.T., Palmer, R.C. Refles (reference librarian enhancement system): a proposal for microcomputer based database for fact retrieval and search strategy development. IN: ASIS proceedings. ASIS annual meeting, Minneapolis, 1979.

Descriptors: Databases: inhouse; information retrieval; reference management

REPORTERM

Supplier: Legal Technology Group
58 South Eaton Place, London, SW1W 9JJ, UK
Tel: 01 730 8040

Hardware: BBC

Requirements: Full duplex modem

Price: Less than 200 pounds sterling with modem

Notes: Aids online access to BBC Wold Reporter database. Operates at 1200/75 baud

Descriptors: Online access to BBC World Reporter database

REVITEL

Supplier: Remidex Office Automation BV
Postbus 20062, 7302 HB Apeldoorn, The Netherlands

Operating System: PC DOS; MS DOS

Hardware: IBM PC

Price: 975 dfl

Notes: The software enables communication between PCs as well as between PC and mainframe. The mainframe can be either a scrolling mode computer such as the international hosts dialog, ESA IRS, or it can be a videotex computer. REVITEL permits the storage of communications protocols and allows uploading, downloading, ending the connection and displaying the results. Access to local area networks, electronic mail and telex systems are possible.

Descriptors: Communications; electronic mail; online search aid; viewdata: access to remote systems

ROTHINES INDEXING AND ABSTRATING SOFTWARE

Supplier: Rothines Associates, Harold Roth and Theodore C. Hines
1113 Hill Street, Greensboro, NC 27408, USA

Operating System: CP/M 2.2

Requirements: Any microcomputer with the Z80 microprocessor

Notes: Creates indexes and abstracts in camera ready copy

Descriptors: Abstracts; indexes

SABINI

Supplier: Organizacion de Consultores, SA
Ramon de la Cruz 39-1æ, 28001- Madrid, Spain
Tel: 431.72.41

Operating System: PICK; Revelation

Hardware: IBM PC XT; IBM PC AT; IBM PC compatibles

Requirements: Hard disk (1 Mb is required for every 1000 records on average)

Price: 24,370 pounds sterling

Notes: SABINI is an integrated local library system which supports library functions using MARC format for bibliographic description. The acquisitions subsystem integrates with the bibliographic database and offers financial control and the ability to set up a supplier file. A thesaurus and authority module is available for use with the catalogue. The catalogue database may be searched using boolean logic. "Select", "combine" and "limit" commands are available, and both right hand and left hand truncation are supported. Various output formats are permitted to either paper, microform or magnetic tape. A circulation module is also available.

Descriptors: Acquisitions; catalogues; catalogues: online; issue system; thesaurus control

SC 350

Supplier: OCLC
6565 Frantz Road, Dublin, OH 43017, USA
Tel: (614) 764-6000

Operating System: PC DOS

Hardware: IBM PC; OCLC M300 workstation
Requirements: Hard disk
Notes: SC350 may be used in association with online data sources such as OCLC's online system or can be fully integrated with standalone library systems. It may also be operated independently as a complete standalone system. The package can support up to 20,000 serials titles. MARC data can be downloaded or brief bibliographic records may be created at the terminal. Records from all sources can be edited. Other features include: check-in; duplicates control; routing; claiming; bindery and subcription control. Current fund balances as well as committed accounts are available. A file of suppliers, agents, publishers and other libraries can be maintained and searched. Several reports may be generated, including financial reports, daily check-in lists, statistical reports on numbers and costs of subscriptions within certain categories, and listings from the bibliographic file. Password protection is available.
Descriptors: MARC interface; serials control

SCI MATE
Supplier: Institue for Scientific Information (USA)
3501 Market Street, University City Science Center, Philadelphia, PA 19104, USA
Notes: See other entry

SCI MATE
Supplier: Capital Systems Group Inc
11301 Rockville PIke, Kensington, MD 20895, USA
Tel: 301 881 9400
Notes: See other entry

SCI MATE
Supplier: Institute for Scientific Information, (UK)
132 High Street, Uxbridge, Middx, UB8 1DP, UK
Tel: 0895-30085
Notes: See other entry

SCI MATE
Supplier: Citech Ltd
PO. Box 5, Ickenham, Uxbridge, Middlesex, UB10 8AF, UK
Tel: 0895 34327
Operating System: CP M; CP M-86; PC DOS; TRS DOS
Hardware: Apple IIe; Apple II Plus; IBM PC; IBM PC XT; TRS 80 model II; TRS 80 model 12; Vector 3; Vector 4; Kaypro 4; Kaypro 10
Requirements: SCI MATE will operate on other CP/M microcomputers with modem and printer
Notes: Two packages in tandem, the SEARCHER and the MANAGER, to aid online search from Dialog, BRS, ISI and Medline and to generate reports from the downloaded data. May be used with BITS. The Manager allows the user to set up own database of retrieved data or local information and offers advanced searching and sorting capabilities. Can operate with SCI MATE EDITOR.
Review: Lundeen, G. and Tenopir, C., Microcomputer software for in-house databases (four top packages under 2000 pounds sterling). Online 9 (5) 1985, pp30-38.
Descriptors: Database: inhouse; information retrieval; online access to BRS; online access to Dialog; online access to ISI; online·access to Medline; online search aid; commercial database subsets

SCI MATE EDITOR
Supplier: Institute for Scientific Information (UK)
132 High Street, Uxbridge, Middx, UB8 1DP, UK
Tel: 0895-30085
Notes: See other entry

SCI MATE EDITOR
Supplier: Institute for Scientific Information (USA)
3501 Market Street, University City Science Center, Philadelphia, PA 19104, USA
Operating System: PC DOS; CP M; MS DOS
Hardware: IBM PC; IBM PC XT; IBM PC AT; IBM PC compatibles
Notes: The EDITOR formats references in fifteen styles supplied with the program, including those required by the American Medical Association and the editor of Nature and Science. Users may also design their own styles. Bibliographic data can be entered at the keyboard or imported from other software. The users design the page layout and specify printer effects like boldface and italics. EDITOR offers five sort options including author sorts in chronological and reverse chronological order. It also embeds the abbreviated references in a manuscript prepared with a word processor. It will then sort the bibliography in the order in which the references are cited in the paper. The EDITOR is the third part of the suite of SCI MATE software. Each component works alone or in combination with the other components.
Descriptors: Bibliographies; reference management

SCOLAS
Supplier: Small Library Computing
48 Lawrence Ave, Holbrook, NY 11741, USA
Tel: 516 588 1387
Operating System: CP/M 2.2+
Requirements: Microcomputers with 8080, Z80 or 8085 processors. Minimum 64K RAM, 100K disk drive, ZA Zenith data systems VDU and printer
Notes: An acquisitions system which can manage up to 64,000 records if adequate disk space
Descriptors: Acquisitions

SEARCH HELPER
Supplier: Information Access Company IAC, Contact Blodwen Tarter,
11 Davis Drive, Belmont, CA 94002, USA
Hardware: Apple II; Apple IIe; Apple II Plus; Eagle IIe; IBM PC; IBM PC XT
Price: 1950 US dollars
Notes: Access to IAC's online databases on Dialog. Searches may be formulated offline. The search packet subscription fixes the price of each search to one low rate which includes the cost of accessing the database, telecommunications costs and the cost of downloading the first 20 citations retrieved. See also DATALINK.
Review: Search helper: the Queen's borough experience, Online, November 1985, pp 53-56

Descriptors: Online access to IAC

SEARCH MASTER

Supplier: SDC Information Services
2500 Colorado Avenue, Santa Monica, CA 90406, USA
Tel: 213 453 6194

Hardware: Apple II; Burroughs B 20; IBM PC; IBM PC compatibles
Requirements: Minimum 128K RAM, communications interface, disk drive, communications cable and modem. For autodial capability use Hayes smartmodem or Hayes compatible.
Notes: Provides for generation and storage of search instructions, and allows easy editing and revision of scripts to be used online. Autodials directly to the host computer or to a Telenet, Tymnet, Datapac or Uninet number on ORBIT, BRS, NLM and Dow Jones. Performs automatic logon, accesses user selected databases on specified systems, automatically responds to ORBIT retrieval system questions, executes pre-established instructions and records all user entries or ORBIT search master script entries in a search log. Post search facilities include storing all user interaction with the retrieval system as a script, editing of search output and building reports from search logs using commercial word processing software. Provides input to other systems. Currently only available in the U.S.
Descriptors: Online access to SDC; online access to BRS; online access to Medline; online access to Dow Jones; online search aid

SEARCHLIT

Supplier: Medisoft
Medical Professions Building, 1595 Soquel Drive, Suite 350, Santa Cruz, CA 95065, USA
Tel: 408 476 7106

Operating System: DOS 1.1; DOS 2.0
Hardware: IBM PC
Requirements: Minimum 128K RAM and disk drive
Price: 149.50 US dollars
Notes: Filing and cross referencing program for a personal literature collection of about 750 references
Descriptors: Reference management

SEARCHLIT 2.0

Supplier: Medisoft
Medical Professions Building, 1595 Soquel Drive, Suite 350, Santa Cruz, CA 95065, USA
Tel: 408 476 7106

Operating System: DOS 1.1; DOS 2.0
Hardware: IBM PC; IBM PC compatibles
Requirements: Minimum 128K RAM, 2 disk drives printer (parallel) optional
Price: 249.50 US dollars. Demonstration disk 10 dollars
Notes: An upgrade of SEARCHLIT 1.1, a filing and cross reference program. Features include a file structure tailored to hard disk operation for larger bibliographic collections, and word processing with line folding and screen editing functions for the creation of abstract text files of unlimited size. Search and retrieval by indexed keywords or string search of author, title and source fields as well as free text searching are possible. Other features include sorted output with format options for bibliographic generation, and the merging of downloaded files as well as other files produced by standard word processors.
Descriptors: Abstracts; reference management; word processing

SEEKEASY

Supplier: Correlation Systems
81 Rockinghorse Road, Ranch Palos Verdes, CA 90274, USA
Tel: 213 833 3462

Operating System: CP/M 2.0; CP/M 2.1; CP/M 2.2
Price: 235 US dollars. Demo disk plus manual for 15 US dollars
Notes: A free form information filing and retrieval program based on a system of menus. SEEKEASY's main functions include searching for a requested item, storing of items, listing of currently stored items, checking file space, packing the data file, editing and printing. Each item can be up to 150 characters long, and the file can contain up to 4 million characters. Any word fragment may be used as a search term, and items which match most closely are retrieved.
Review: Vogt, Sjoerd "SEEKEASY" The Electronic Library 2 (4) October 1984 pp237-238
Descriptors: Databases: inhouse; information retrieval

SERIALS MANAGEMENT SYSTEM: SMS

Supplier: Serials Management Services Ltd
Cannon House, Folkestone, Kent, CT19 5EE, UK
Tel: 0303 57421; tlx: 96392

Operating System: PC DOS
Hardware: IBM PC; IBM PC compatibles
Price: 2,250 pounds sterling to Dawson customers, 2,750 pounds sterling to non-customers. An additional 400 pounds sterling annual maintenance charge.
Notes: Software package offering: check-in with claiming and routing slip functions; browse and enquiry on orders, reader/circulation and claim status; printing of orders to suppliers, reader analysis, fund/cost code analysis, and claims; online enquiry on title/publisher to Dawson database, message service and electronic ordering and claiming; and total system security. Communication via PSS, SPNS or a private line is also possible. The system may be networked to provide a multi-user facility. Interlibrary loan and binding modules are under development.
Descriptors: Communications; serials control

SILICON OFFICE

Supplier: Bristol Software Factory Ltd
Southfield House, Southfield Road, Westbury-on-Trym, Bristol, BS9 3BH, UK
Tel: 0272 629790; tlx: 946240 cweasy g

Operating System: MS DOS; Commodore DOS
Hardware: Apricot; Commodore 8096; Commodore 8032; DEC personal computers; IBM PC; IBM PC XT; Sirius; Victor 9000
Requirements: Victor 9000 minimum 256K RAM
Price: 790 pounds sterling

Notes: An integrated word processing, information storage and retrieval, report generator and spread sheet package. Offers programming facilities and text editing. Also performs calculations. Includes an optional communications ability using Commodore 8010 modems at 300 baud, allowing two way communication between SILICON OFFICE systems over telephone lines. Supports 64,000 records of 254 bytes maximum. (Version 2 now available).

Review: PC User May 1984 pp 53-60

Descriptors: Administration; communications; information retrieval; word processing

SIR

Supplier: Research Machines Ltd
Mill Street, Oxford, OX2 0BW, UK

Operating System: CP/M 2.2

Hardware: Research Machines 380Z; Research Machines 480Z

Requirements: Microcomputers may be networked together using the chain network

Price: 60 pounds sterling. Free with networks in education

Notes: Schools Information Retrieval project trials have shown successful use of the package for a variety of curricular purposes including project work, careers and library use

Review: McElroy, A.R. Barclay, K. "SIR. Library oriented information processing package for operation on a microcomputer" Program 15 (4) October 1981 pp 233-237

Descriptors: Information retrieval; school libraries

SIRE

Supplier: Software Consulting Services
Ben Franklin Technology Center 125, Suite 10, Murray H. Goodman Campus, Lehigh University, Bethlehem, PA 18015, USA
Tel: 215 861 7920

Operating System: PC DOS

Hardware: IBM PC; IBM PC XT

Price: 90 US dollars for demonstration disk

Notes: Full text automatic indexing system, with features such as Boolean operators and truncation. Requests are entered in natural language. Retrieved articles are ranked according to relevance, and a barchart is displayed to show this. Search terms will be highlighted in the article on the screen. The roots of words are used for searching, allowing the user to find the variants of a word. The alpha command shows the root forms of the words in the database, and will display the 10 words before and the 10 words after the requested word alphabetically. SIRE has an automatic thesaurus. Fields may be user defined and it is possible to select which fields will be displayed and searched.

Review: Lundeen, G. and Tenopir C., Microcomputer software for in-house databases (four top packages under 2000 pounds sterling). Online 9 (5) 1985, pp30-38

Descriptors: Databases: inhouse; information retrieval; thesaurus control

SMART TERMINAL

Supplier: Howe Software
14 Lexington Road, New City, NY 10956, USA
Tel: 914 634 1821

Operating System: CP M

Hardware: TRS 80 model I; TRS 80 model II; TRS 80 model III; TRS 80 model IV; TRS 80 model 12

Requirements: Smart terminal can be mounted on other CP/M microcomputers

Price: 74.95 US dollars (TRS 80 model I, III, IV); 79.95 US dollars (TRS 80 models II, 12 and CP/M micros)

Notes: Intelligent telecommunications program. Allows the micro to be used as a terminal to information systems, time sharing computers, or for data transmission and reception. Data files are compatible with Electric Pencil and Scripsit, and other word processing packages. Back up copies may be created.

Descriptors: Communications

SMARTCOM II

Supplier: Hayes Microcomputer Products Inc
5923 Peachtree Industrial Blvd., Norcross, Georgia 30092, USA
Tel: 404/442 1617; tlx: 703500 hayes usa

Hardware: Apple Macintosh; DEC Rainbow; HP 150; IBM PC; IBM PC compatibles; TI professional; Wang professional

Requirements: Hayes smartmodem

Notes: SMARTCOM II provides error-free communications with Hayes verification and xmodem protocols. It is possible to record up to 25 messages, files or letters at a time and transmit them at night when phone rates are low. The software stores telephone numbers, log on procedures and communications protocols which can be later executed with a few keystrokes. Other features include: on-screen password protection; data capture at the press of a key; the printing of data while recording it to disk; voice to data transmission, and the emulation of DEC VT100 and VT52 terminals.

Descriptors: Communications; online search aid

SPINE POCKET CARD LABELS PROGRAM

Supplier: Library Processes System
919 West Canadian Street, Vinita, Oklahoma 74301, USA
Tel: 918 256 8598

Hardware: TRS 80 model III; TRS 80 model IV

Price: 125 US dollars

Notes: Each entry produces two spine labels and two author/title labels, one for the pocket and the other for the borrower's card. All labels include: type; classification number; author letters; volume or copy number. The program is for use with the library processes system card catalog and utilises data already entered and stored from that program.

Descriptors: Labels

STAR

Supplier: Cuadra Associates Inc
2001 Wilshire Blvd., Suite 305, Santa Monica, CA 90403, USA
Tel: 213 829 9972
Operating System: CP M
Hardware: Alpha Microsystems Business Computer
Requirements: IBM PC or IBM PC compatibles as terminals to the Alpha micro; Alpha micro/PC upgrade package for multi-user operation
Price: 20,900+ US dollars with hardware; from 2,550 dollars for upgrade package
Notes: An integrated database development and information retrieval system. Up to 1000 databases of over 250 million characters may be defined. Data may be entered with full screen text editing capabilities. Boolean searches are possible from an inverted index. Truncation, nested parentheses, field qualification and index viewing are available. Records may contain up to 2 million characters, and there can be as many 500 fields per record.
Review: Cuadra, N.G. "STAR: a microcomputer system for data entry, retrieval and publication support." Electronic Publishing Review 1 (2) pp 131-138; "Searching one million records on digital laser discs" Library Hi Tech News No. 14 March 1985 p1,8
Descriptors: Databases: inhouse; information retrieval

STRIX

Supplier: Kent Barlow Information Associates
Kingsmead House, 250 Kings Road, Chelsea, London, SW3 5UE, UK
Tel: 01 351 2776; tlx: 268627
Operating System: Uniflex
Hardware: SWTPc S09
Requirements: Minimum 128K RAM, dual 8" floppy disk system or hard disk and 80 column printer
Price: 950 pounds sterling. 1045 pounds sterling with microfilm retrieval software.
Notes: STRIX provides the facility to create one or more textual databases, each with its own structure defined by the user. Each record may contain up to 50 separately identifiable fields which may be defined as occuring once only in each record, or many times. Fields may contain up to 255 characters. There is a prompted data input facility. Record and field deletion, insertion of additional data and editing of existing data are possible. The system allows searching on any field, any logical combination of words or word prefixes. Search results may be displayed at the terminal or routed to a printer. STRIX is menu driven software and screens are cursor controlled. STRIX can be linked to a microfilm reader printer. Record size up to 32,000 characters.
Descriptors: Databases: inhouse; information retrieval

SURVEYS

Supplier: Mr. Craig
209 Nelson Court East, Madison, TN 37115, USA
Hardware: TRS 80 model II
Price: On application
Descriptors: Administration: survey analysis

SWIFT

Supplier: Kent Barlow Information Associates
Kingsmead House, 250 Kings Road, Chelsea, London, SW3 5UE, UK
Tel: 01 351 2776; tlx: 26862
Operating System: CP M
Hardware: Altos; BBC; Cifer 2684; Cromenco; Columbia; IBM PC; Superbrain; Sirius
Requirements: SWIFT may be adapted to other CP/M machines.
Price: 225 pounds sterling
Notes: See MAGPIE
Descriptors: Online search aid

SX 350

Supplier: OCLC Europe
2nd Floor, Lloyds Bank Chambers, 75 Edmund Street, Birmingham, B3 3HA, UK
Tel: 021 236 3224/5; tlx: 335176 oclc tfstrs g
Operating System: PC DOS
Hardware: IBM PC; OCLC M300 workstation
Requirements: Hard disk
Notes: SC 350 may be used in association with online data sources such as OCLC's online system or can be fully integrated with standalone library systems. It may also be operated independently as a complete standalone system. The package can support up to 20,000 serials titles. MARC data can be downloaded or brief bibliographic records may be created at the terminal. Records from all sources can be edited. Other features include: check-in; duplicates control; routing; claiming; bindery and subscription control. Current fund balances as well as committed accounts are available. A file of suppliers, agents, publishers and other libraries can be maintained and searched. Several reports may be generated, including financial reports, daily check-in lists, statistical reports on numbers and costs of subscriptions within certain categories, and listings from the bibliographic file. Password protection is available.
Descriptors: MARC interface; serials control

SYDNEY'S MICRO LIBRARY SYSTEM

Notes: See MICROLIBRARY

TAMIL

Supplier: Tamil
91 Bd Edmmond Rostand, 95500 Rueil Malmaison, France
Tel: 47323534; tlx: 270105F txfra/ref 345
Operating System: UNIX
Hardware: ONYX C 8002; Fortune; Thompson Micromega 32; Plexus; Unixsys; NCT Tower
Price: 7000 to 15,000 US dollars
Notes: The TAMIL system is designed for documentation centres and libraries which possess from 5,000 to 1,000,000 documents. The software offers online input of alphanumeric and numeric data. Record lengths are variable. A maximum record length of 3200 characters is allowed, and the system supports up to 400,000 records with 100 fields per record. Editing facilities are available. The software allows Boolean searching, numerical searching, search term truncation, field based and full text searching, nested search terms, alternative query languages and synonyms. The package

supports catalogue and circulation functions. A print generator is available. System command language is in French and English and documentation is available in French and English. System allows uploading and downloading and duplicate entries check. It is sold as MICRO QUESTEL by Telesystemes Questel.
Descriptors: Catalogues; databases: inhouse; information retrieval; issue system

TANDATA VIEWTEX MICROPACK

Supplier: Tandata Marketing Ltd
Albert Rd North, Malvern, Worcester, WR14 2TL, UK
Tel: 06845 68421; tlx: 337617
Operating System: MS DOS; PC DOS 2.1+; CP M-86; CP M
Hardware: Selected micros
Notes: A menu driven viewdata/videotex package featuring autodial and autologon to databases, the saving to disk of messages, pages or forms which can be recalled and displayed automatically at preset intervals. An editor permits the creation of files or messages for transmission. Print facilities are available. The system is for use with Prestel or private viewdata, and for many conventional databases such as Telecom Gold.
Descriptors: Online search aid; viewdata: inhouse systems; viewdata: access to remote systems

TELEMARC III

Supplier: Gaylord Bros Inc
P.O. Box 4901, Syracuse, NY 13221, USA
Tel: 800 448 6160
Hardware: Franklin Ace; Apple II plus; Apple IIe
Requirements: Minimum 48K RAM, 5.25" disk drives, lower case adaptor and printer
Price: 595 US dollars
Notes: Produces catalogue cards, pocket and spine labels. Designed for small to medium sized libraries. The operator prepares a main entry card and the system produces a fully headed card set and label set. The entered data is automatically formatted, and up to 45 fields are permitted per card. A batch printing feature is included which allows for unattended printing of catalogue entries. The system is menu driven with a series of user prompts.
Descriptors: Catalogue cards; labels

TELEPEN LIBRARY SYSTEM

Supplier: S B Electronic Systems Ltd
Arden Grove, Harpenden, Herts, AL5 4SL, UK
Tel: 05827 69991
Hardware: Telepen system 4
Notes: Intelligent data capture terminals with full circulation control using barcode readers
Descriptors: Issue system

TEQLIB

Supplier: Software Consulting Services
Ben Franklin Technology Center·125, Suite 10, Murray H. Goodman Campus, Lehigh University, Bethlehem, PA 18015, USA
Tel: 215 861 7920
Hardware: IBM PC; IBM PC XT; Apple II; TRS 80 model II
Price: 1500 US dollars; 25 dollars for manual; 500 dollars per annum maintenance; demonstration disk 60 dollars
Notes: Textual retrieval system designed to hold full text articles or abstracts for journalists and researchers. Articles are indexed by user generated key phrases and access is available by author, subject, keyphrase or date. The system can also retrieve articles by entering only part of the key, or phonetic approximation of an author's last name. It has a "see also" facility. In conjunction with a printer, the system also provides various reports as hard copy, indexes of all authors and key phrases in the database. It handles up to 50,000 or 100,000 abstracts with hard disk.
Descriptors: Databases: inhouse; information retrieval; indexes; reference management

TERM MARC

Supplier: Small Library Computing
48 Lawrence Ave, Holbrook, NY 11741, USA
Tel: 516 588 1387
Operating System: PC DOS 2.0+
Hardware: IBM PC; IBM PC XT; IBM PC AT
Requirements: Minimum 192K RAM and 2 disk drives
Price: 195 US dollars
Notes: A utility program for use with the OCLC M300 workstation. Processes records saved to disk and reformats them into full MARC records. The records can then be loaded into systems which use the MARC format. Several auxiliary programs useful in manipulating, validating and listing files of MARC records are also included.
Descriptors: Catalogues; data formatting; MARC interface; retrospective conversion

TESTMAGIC

Supplier: Head Computers Ltd
Oxted Mill, Spring Lane, Oxted, Surrey, RH8 9PB, UK
Tel: 08833 7057/5580; tlx: 957525 oxmill g
Price: 60 pounds sterling plus VAT
Notes: A low cost evaluation version of the INMAGIC information storage and retrieval software. TESTMAGIC includes all the features of INMAGIC, but holds up to 50 records in each test file. These features include variable field lengths and records, nested Boolean, range and text word searching, interactive and batch database updating, and user defined databases, report formats and sequences.
Descriptors: Databases: inhouse; information retrieval

TEXTO

Supplier: Chemdata SA
Tour Saone-Croix-Rouge, 17 Quai Joseph Gillet, 69316 Lyon, France
Tel: 7 829 7055
Notes: See entry for PINDOC

THESAURUS

Supplier: Pyramid Computer Systems Ltd
9 Church Street, Reading, Berkshire RG1 2SB, UK
Tel: (0734)595633; tlx: 848278 gilco g
Operating System: MS DOS; PC DOS; CP/M-80
Price: 195 pounds sterling (plus VAT)
Notes: Stand-alone software for the online creation and maintenance of thesauri. Both an alphabetical and subject display are maintained online and printed if required. Broader, narrower and related terms are supported with see also, seen from, preferred terms and scope notes. When a term relationship is entered the reverse relationship is automatically assigned, and the total number of relationships for that term is displayed. May be used with CALM.
Descriptors: Thesaurus control

TIN: The Information Navigator

Supplier: Informationsberatung
Gruppellostrasse 13, 4000 Dusseldorf 1, West Germany
Tel: 211 364 317
Notes: See other entry

TIN: The Information Navigator

Supplier: Informazione Facile
CP 237, 5510, Firenze, Italy
Tel: 055 697509
Notes: See other entry

TIN: THE INFORMATION NAVIGATOR

Supplier: Information Management and Engineering Ltd
1, Carthusian Street, London, EC1M 6EB, UK
Tel: 01 253 1177
Operating System: MS DOS 2.x; PC DOS 2.x; MS DOS 2.0+
Hardware: IBM PC; IBM PC compatibles
Requirements: Minimum 512K RAM over 300K RAM and a minimum of 20Mb hard disk storage is recommended
Price: From 500 to 2500 pounds sterling for single-user systems. Multi-user software costs from 1000 pounds sterling more
Notes: TINMAN is a database management/information retrieval system which has the ability to receive, record, store and correlate data of all kinds. Records and field lengths are unlimited and there can be as many variable length fields as desired. Data can be retrieved by "browsing" through ordered lists of information and then "navigating" to something of interest by pressing one key when the relevant item appears. Word and string searching are permitted; Boolean operators can be used and retrieved sets saved for printing or further manipulation. Data may be be keyed directly to the system or downloaded from machine-readable files. TINMAN has a full screen-based editor. Messages, help screens and the keyboard, including function keys, can be changed by the user if desired. The software can handle multiple languages simultaneously, including non-Roman languages. It has a full thesaurus capability including links between thesauri and multi-lingual thesauri. Applications include: library systems; conference information and management; thesaurus construction; project information and management; records management, and the handling of archives and manuscripts collections. There is sophisticated access control and a password system.
Review: Noerr, P.L. and Noerr, K.T.B. Browse and navigate: an advance in database access methods. Information processing and management, 21 (3) 1985, pp205-213 Aslib information - Sept 1986; Information world review Sept 1986; Biblioteche oggi - Feb 1986
Descriptors: Databases: inhouse; information retrieval; thesaurus control

TOP CLASS

Supplier: Ctrl. Alt. Deli
44 Brownbaker Court, Neath Hill, Milton Keynes, Buckinghamshire, MK14 6JH, UK
Hardware: IBM PC; IBM PC XT; IBM PC compatibles
Notes: TOP CLASS is designed for the production of computer-based tutorials, presentations, interviews and consultations. Information may be presented using a combination of text, colour, graphics, sound and movement. The menu-driven program generator allows the new user to begin production immediately. Practised users can make full use of the 30 commands which cover the elements of information presentation, question handling and session control. Messages and commands can be sent down the serial port of the PC at any time during the session. This can be used for keeping a supervisor informed of progress, or to control external equipment.
Descriptors: User education

TPS 400 ONLINE INTERFACE

Supplier: TPS Electronics
4047 Transport Street, Palo Alto, CA 94303, USA
Tel: 415 856 6833
Operating System: Apple DOS
Hardware: Apple IIe
Requirements: Minimum 48K RAM
Price: 10,000 US dollars
Notes: The TPS 400 ONLINE INTERFACE serves as an intelligent buffer memory between an online cataloguing system such as OCLC or RLIN and an online circulation system such as CL Systems Inc's libs-100. MARC records are reformatted and then transmitted to the circulation computer with the necessary additional data, such as alphabetic identifiers, added. TPS 400 can be provide combined with the TPS-300 barcode reader interface, to provide one step processing for new material.
Descriptors: Data formatting; issue system; retrospective conversion

TPS 450 ONLINE SPINE LABEL PRINTING SYSTEM

Supplier: TPS Electronics
4047 Transport Street, Palo Alto, CA 94303, USA
Tel: 415 856 6833
Hardware: Apple IIe
Price: 6500 US dollars

Notes: The spine label printing system provides online printing of spine and pocket labels from rlin or oclc catalogue records. Labels may be printed immediately or transferred to floppy disk for later printing. Labels may be printed offline and sorted by the initiating terminal so that groups of labels and books are kept together. Manual data input may also be utilized for off-line label production.
Descriptors: Labels

TTY
Supplier: MVA Systematica
MVA House, Victoria Way, Woking, Surrey, GU2 1DD, UK
Tel: 04862 28051
Operating System: CP M; CP M-86; MS DOS
Price: 140 pounds sterling
Notes: Communications program that allows a micro to act as an intelligent terminal to a variety of host computers. Supports up and downloading.
Descriptors: Communications; online search aid

ULTRACARD
Supplier: Capital Systems Group Inc
11301 Rockville Pike Kensington, Maryland 20895, USA
Tel: 301 881 9400
Notes: See other entry

ULTRACARD
Supplier: Small Library Computing
48 Lawrence Ave, Holbrook, NY 11741, USA
Tel: 516 588 1387
Operating System: PC DOS 1.1; PC DOS 2.0; Z DOS; MS DOS
Hardware: IBM PC; IBM PC XT; Zenith Z100
Requirements: Minimum 128K RAM, disk drive and printer
Price: 495 US dollars
Notes: Prints catalogue cards and card, pocket and spine labels which can be printed in several formats. Version 3 permits the creation of sorted and paginated bibliographies from the cataloguing records, and the system supports the input and printing of foreign language diacritics. Version 3 allows up to 50 lines of information as opposed to the 20 lines supported by version 2. Notes may be included in the cataloguing record.
Descriptors: Catalogue cards; labels

ULTRACARD MARC
Supplier: Small Library Computing
48 Lawrence Ave, Holbrook, NY 11741, USA
Tel: 516 588 1387
Operating System: PC DOS 2.0+
Hardware: IBM PC; IBM PC XT; IBM PC AT
Requirements: Minimum 192K RAM, 2 disk drives and a printer
Price: 595 US dollars
Notes: Similar to ULTRACARD, but allows the entry of a full MARC record including the fixed fields, indicators and subfield codes. Supports books, serials, AV materials, archival and manuscript control, maps, music and machine readable data files. May be used for retrospective conversion.
Descriptors: Archive control; audio-visual control; catalogue cards; retrospective conversaion

UNICORN COLLECTION MANAGEMENT SYSTEM
Supplier: Sirsi Corporation
8106 B South Memorial Parkway, Huntsville, Alabama 35802, USA
Tel: 205 881 2140
Operating System: UNIX
Notes: Sirsi's UNICORN COLLECTION MANAGEMENT SYSTEM is a fully integrated library system with bibliographic, public access, circulation academic reserves, acquisitions, serials control, bulletin board and electronic mail modules. Modules can be configured as separate systems or integrated on one system. A unique user interface gives simultaneous access to all system commands. UNICORN can be purchased for single or multiple access points. Cooperating libraries can also network UNICORN systems. Both barcode readers and full alphanumeric OCR wands can be used optionally with the UNICORN system. Direct interfaces to laser disk (lasertap), OCLC (datatap) and other cataloguing sources are available to enable the librarian to transfer records from these sources directly to the UNICORN. UNIX based unicorn runs on anything from PCs to mainframes. It is available as a turnkey system combining software and hardware, or as a software only package for UNIX computers.
Review: Microcomputer based circulation: Sirsi Corporation's UNICORN system. Library Hi Tech (1) PP44-46; Library Software Review vol.3, No1,; Library Software Review Sept-Oct, 1985 pp 271-273.
Descriptors: Acquisitions; bulletin board; catalogues; electronic mail; issue system; serials control

UNIVERSITY OF MINNESOTA PERIODICALS MANAGEMENT
Supplier: University of Minnesota
Duluth, MN 55812, USA
Hardware: Terak
Descriptors: Serials control

VICOM
Supplier: A.M. Computer Technology Ltd
16 Kensington Court Place, London, W8 5BJ, UK
Operating System: Apple DOS 3.3
Hardware: Apple II Plus; Apple IIe; Apple IIc
Requirements: Modem
Notes: VICOM is a communications software package which permits a microcomputer to access viewdata and ASCII/text databases, as well as to send and receive telexes and electronic mail. The package is menu-driven and includes a help facility. Communication speeds of 75/1200, 300/300,1200/75 and 1200/1200 baud are permitted, and the software supports both X-on/X-off flow control and X-modem transmission protocols. The user may program log-on sequences for access to remote databases, and autodial is supported with certain modems. Data may be downloaded to disk or routed to

a printer. Files may be transferred from one apple to another.
Descriptors: Communications; electronic mail; online search aid; viewdata: access to remote systems

VIDACCESS
Supplier: Information Intelligence Inc.
P.O. Box 31098, Phoenix, AZ 85046, USA
Tel: (800) 228-9982 (except Arizona & Alaska); (602) 996-2283
Operating System: DOS 3.3
Hardware: Apple II; Apple II Plus; Apple IIe
Requirements: Minimum 48K RAM; two apple 5.25" disk drive; clock card, Hayes or Hayes-compatibles 300 or 1200 baud modem; supports Apple 80-column cards for Apple IIe.
Price: 2,500,00 US dollars
Notes: VIDACCESS is a modified A-C-C-E-S-S (tm) "read only" online system which offers up to 100 lines of text per message. There is no networking capability for this version. Three add-on programs (25 dollars each - all three for 50 dollars) include System Name, Auto-Delete, and Auxiliary File. (See A-C-C-E-S-S). (References to this product in Rorvig, M.E., Microcomputers and Libraries, are inaccurate).
Descriptors: Bulletin boards; communications; interlibrary loans; electronic mail; viewdata: access to remote systems.

VIDEO LIBRARY SYSTEM
Supplier: Vista Systems Ltd
82/84 Crabtree Lane, Lancing, West Sussex BN15 9PJ, UK
Tel: 0903 750711
Hardware: Tandon PCX20
Price: 2950+ pounds sterling including hardware, installation and training
Notes: A computerised video library management system, capable of handling up to 10,000 films and 10,000 users. Upgradable to a multi user system, using the Novel Network Operating System. Main functions include member and film files, bookings and reservations, fee calculations, overdues statistics and audit files.
Descriptors: Audio visual control

VISILINK
Supplier: Visicorp
2895 Zanke Road, San Jose, CA 95134, USA
Notes: Searches DRI database. Statistical sources can be converted for further manipulation with Visitrend.
Descriptors: Online access to DRI database

WILSEARCH
Supplier: H.W. Wilson Software Company
950 University Avenue, Bronx, New York 10452, USA
Tel: 212 588 8400
Operating System: DOS 2.0+
Hardware: IBM PC; IBM PC XT; IBM PC AT; IBM PC compatibles
Notes: The WILSEARCH software allows searches to be formulated offline using menus. The searches are then uploaded to the Wilson online databases, two of which may be searched simultaneously if required. More detailed help information may be requested at any time and a "help" window explains the options available at any point during the search formulation. The software is currently available only in the USA.
Descriptors: Online search aid; online access to Wilson

WILSONDISC
Supplier: The H.W. Wilson Software Company
950 University Ave, Bronx, NY 10452, USA
Tel: (212) 588-8400
Operating System: PC DOS 3.1
Hardware: IBM PC XT
Requirements: 640K RAM, colour card and monitor, pro printer and card, Hitachi or Philips CD-ROM player
Notes: The WILSONDISC system offers access to bibliographic data on CD-ROM, via a choice of four access modes: browse, offering access to Wilson subject headings and the same entry capabilities as the printed indexes; Wilsearch, offering the Wilsearch capabilities on the WILSONDISC; Wilsonline, which incorporates the same search capabilities as the Wilsonline database; expert mode which offers the same capabilities as Wilsonline, but with expanded screen handling and windowing functions.
Descriptors: Information retrieval: commercial database subsets

XMODEM PC
Supplier: BVR Vedder
Weissenburger Str. 16, D-8546 Thalmessing, W. Germany
Tel: 9173/1216
Operating System: PC DOS 2.0+; MS DOS 2.0+
Hardware: IBM PC; IBM PC compatibles
Requirements: Monochrome, Hercules or EGA card, serial port and modem (DATAPHON S21-23d recommended)
Price: Less than 100 DM
Notes: A telecommunications package which can operate between 110 and 9600 baud. Files may be up or downloaded using either Xon/Xoff protocol or the Xmodem protocol of Ward Christensen. The built-in editor works with Wordstar commands and allows two files to be edited at the same time using a window technique. Up to 40 commands or strings, each of up to 72 characters may be stored under function keys to enable easy storage and transmission of passwords and search terms. Comments are issued in German.
Descriptors: Communications; online search aid

ZEUS
Supplier: Dr Karl Thomas GMBH
Biberach an der Riss, West Germany
Hardware: Wang Office Information System (OIS 140)
Notes: A computerised system for the administration of about 1100 journal subscriptions and the handling of a routing control for approximately 1000 readers. The system caters for check in and claiming procedures, subscription control, binding and statistics. The system is menu driven.
Review: Schmitz, B and Kalbfleisch, W. "ZEUS, a system for serials check in and routing control" IN: Helal, A.H. and Weiss, J.W. Local Library Systems.

Essen Symposium 24-27 September 1984. Essen University 1984
Descriptors: Circulation: serials; serials control

25:02
Supplier: Information Solutions Inc
Softrend Division, PO Box 198,
Charlottesville, Virginia 22902, USA
Tel: 800-368-3452
Operating System: PC DOS
Hardware: IBM PC
Price: 89 US Dollars
Notes: Reference storage and retrieval, allowing: cross reference by publication, author or subject; up to 80 characters abstract; production of bibliographies by publication, author or subject. Each entry contains issue and publication date as well as page number and location of reference. Entries may be added, changed or deleted at any time. There is menu driven function selection and on screen reference to relevant manual sections.
Descriptors: Abstracts; bibliographies; reference management

Abstracts
- RASMUS
- ROTHINES INDEXING AND ABSTRACTING SOFTWARE
- SEARCHLIT 2.0
- 25:02

Access to Remote systems
- ASSIST

Accessions lists
- ACCESSION PLUS
- CARD CATALOG
- LASS
- PROTOKOL

Acquisitions
- ACQUEST
- ADLIB 2
- ALC BASIC LIBRARY SERVICES
- BIB BASE ACQ
- BIB BASE ACQ AND BIB BASE CAT COMBINED
- BIBLIO BUY
- BOOKSHELF
- BOOKTRAK
- CALM : COMPUTER AIDED LIBRARY MANAGEMENT
- CARD DATALOG
- INMAGIC BIBLIO
- INNOVACQ
- INTEGRATED MICROCOMPUTER LIBRARY SYSTEM
- KAMBIS
- LIBRARY MANAGEMENT SYSTEM
- LIBS 100 : SYSTEM 23
- LICON
- LINX
- LIS
- MICROLIBRARY
- NONESUCH ACQUISITIONS SYSTEM
- OCELOT ACQUISITIONS MODULE
- OCELOT LIBRARY SYSTEM
- ORDERIT
- PEARL 4.0
- SABINI
- SCOLAS
- UNICORN COLLECTION MANAGEMENT SYSTEM

Administration
- BITS : BOEING INTELLIGENT TERMINAL SYSTEM
- CORMORANT
- SILICON OFFICE

Administration : Survey analysis
- SURVEYS

Archive control
- MARS : MICROCOMPUTER ARCHIVES AND RECORDS MANAGEMENT SYSTEMS
- ULTRACARD MARC

Audio Visual control
- A V EQUIPMENT INVENTORY
- A V INVENTORY
- ART PRINT INVENTORY
- CIRCULATION MANAGER
- FILM BOOKING
- INTEGRATED MICROCOMPUTER LIBRARY SYSTEM
- MEDIA AND EQUIPMENT MANAGEMENT
- ULTRACARD MARC
- VIDEO LIBRARY SYSTEM

Bibliographies
- ACCESSION PLUS
- BIBLIOGRAPHY COMPILER
- BIBLIOGRAPHY WRITER
- BOOKENDS
- BOOKENDS EXTENDED
- BOOKENDS PRO DOS
- CATALOG CARD PROGRAM
- COMPUTER CAT : MULTI USER
- CURRENT TITLES SYSTEM
- DATA TRANSFER SYSTEM
- INDEXING
- LIBRAMATIX
- NOTA BENE
- PEARL 4.0
- PERSONAL BIBLIOGRAPHIC SYSTEM
- PRO-CITE
- PROFESSIONAL BIBLIOGRAPHIC SYSTEM 2.6
- PROTOKOL
- QUICK SEARCH LIBRARIAN
- SCI MATE EDITOR
- 25:02

Biosciences information services data
- BITS

Book indexes
- ACTA CRYSTALLOGRAPHICA INDEX SYSTEM
- BOOKDEX
- MICROINDEX

Borrower registration
- BORROWERS FILE

Bulletin boards
- ACCESS (TM) — MICROCOMPUTER NETWORK SYSTEM
- LOAN
- UNICORN COLLECTION MANAGEMENT SYSTEM
- VIDACCESS

Catalogue cards
- BIB BASE ACQ AND BIB BASE CATE COMBINED
- BIB BASE CAT
- BOOKTRAK
- CALM 3.1 : CARD AND LABEL MANAGER
- CARD
- CARD CATALOG
- CARDPREP
- CARDPRO : APPLE
- CARDPRO : TRS
- CATALOG CARD AND LABEL WRITER
- CATALOG CARD MAKER III
- CATALOG CARD PROGRAM
- CATALOGIT
- CATALOGUE CARDS
- MICROMARC
- PET COMPUTER LIBRARY CARD MAKER
- PROTOKOL
- TELEMARC III
- ULTRACARD
- ULTRACARD MARC

Catalogues
- BBC MICRO LIBRARY SYSTEM
- BIB BASE
- BIB BASE MARC
- BOOKSHELF
- CALM : COMPUTER AIDED LIBRARY MANAGEMENT
- CARD DATALOG
- CIRCA II
- COMPUTER CAT : MULTI USER
- CORTEX
- CTI
- DYNIX

EAGLE
FICTION FINDER
FOCUS
I-CIRC
INFOQUEST
INMAGIC BIBLIO
INNOVACQ
INTEGRATED MICROCOMPUTER LIBRARY SYSTEM
KAMBIS
KWIRS
LASS
LENDING LIBRARY (THE)
LIBRAMATIX
LIBRARIAN
LIBRARY MANAGEMENT SYSTEM
LICON
LIS
LSSI LASERFILE SYSTEM
MEDICAL LIBRARIAN
METALOGUE
MICROFILE
MICROLIBRARY
MIKRO POLYDOC
MITINET RETRO
OCELOT CATALOGUE MODULE
ORICAT
PEARL 4.0
PROFESSIONAL BIBLIOGRAPHIC SYSTEM 2.6
PROTOKOL
SABINI
TAMIL
TERM MARC
UNICORN COLLECTION MANAGEMENT SYSTEM

Catalogues : audio visual material

A V CATALOG WRITER
AV CARD DIRECTORY PROGRAM

Catalogues : online

ADLIB2
ALC BASIC LIBRARY SERIES
BOOKSHELF
CIRCA II
COMPUTER CAT : MULTI USER
CORTEX
CTI
DYNIX
FICTION FINDER
INFOQUEST
INNOVACQ
INTEGRATED MICROCOMPUTER LIBRARY SYSTEM
KAMBIS
LENDING LIBRARY (THE)
LIBRARIAN
LIBS 100 : SYSTEM 23
LICON
LIS
LSSI LASERFILE SYSTEM
METALOGUE
MICROLIBRARY
OCELOT CATALOGUE MODULE
OCELOT LIBRARY SYSTEM
OPAC ACCESS
PEARL 4.0
SABINI

Circulation : serials

LINX
MICROLINX CHECK-IN
PEARL 4.0
PERIODICALS
ZEUS

CLSI : data entry to

CTI

Communications

ACCESS (TM) — MICROCOMPUTER NETWORK SYSTEM
ASCOM IV
BIBLIO BUY
BITS : BOEING INTELLIGENT TERMINAL SYSTEM
CONNECT
COPYLINK
CROSSTALK
CROSSTALK XVI
DRM TELETYPE EMULATOR
HEADFORM
I & D SOFTWARE
INSTANTCOM ESL
INSTANTCOM 3.1
LIAISON
LSTERM COMMUNICATIONS SOFTWARE
MITE
PC DIAL
POST PLUS
POST PLUS BRIEFCASE
POST PLUS CONCURRENT
RASMUS
REVITEL
SERIALS MANAGEMENT SYSTEM : SMS
SILICON OFFICE
SMART TERMINAL
SMARTCOM II
TTY
VICOM
VIDACCESS
XMODEM PC

Data entry (see also Data input)

BIB BASE MARC
BIBLIO TEL
BITS : BOEING INTELLIGENT TERMINAL SYSTEM
CTI
HEADSET

Data formatting

TERM MARC
TPS 400 ON-LINE INTERFACE

Data input (see also Data entry)

BIB BASE MARC
BIB BASE TEXT

Databases : inhouse

AQUILA
ASSASSIN PC
BITS : BOEING INTELLIGENT TERMINAL SYSTEM
BRS SEARCH
DATAFAX
EAGLE
FACTFINDER
FINDER
GOLDEN RETRIEVER
I
INFOBASE
INMAGIC MICRO
LIBRARY MATE (PREVIOUSLY LIBRARIAN)
MICRO CAIRS
MICRO STATUS
MICROBIRD
MIKRO POLYDOC
MIRABILIS
PINDOC
POPPYTIME INFORMATION RETRIEVAL SYSTEM
PROFESSIONAL BIBLIOGRAPHIC SYSTEM 2.6

QUICK SEARCH LIBRARIAN
RASMUS
RECALL
REFLES : REFERENCE LIBRARIAN ENHANCEMENT SYSTEM
SCI MATE
SEEKEASY
SIRE
STAR
STRIX
TAMIL
TEQLIB
TESTMAGIC
TIN : THE INFORMATION NAVIGATOR

Downloading

DATA TRANSFER SYSTEM

Electronic mail

ACCESS (TM) — MICROCOMPUTER NETWORK SYSTEM
ASSIST
F.I.L.L.S. : FAST INTERLIBRARY LOANS AND STATISTICS
F.I.L.L.S. : FAST INTERLIBRARY LOANS AND STATISTICS 2.0
INFOKOM
INSTANTCOM ESL
INSTANTCOM 3.1
LOAN
LSTERM COMMUNICATIONS SOFTWARE
ON TYME
REVITEL
UNICORN COLLECITON MANAGEMENT SYSTEM
VICOM
VIDACCESS

ERIC database subsets

MICRO SEARCH

Finances

LIBRARY ACCOUNTS
LIBRARY BUDGETS FTE CALC
ONLINE PRICING SIMULATOR

Graphics

BITS : BOEING INTELLIGENT TERMINAL SYSTEM
I & D SOFTWARE
INFOKOM

Indexes

ACTA CRYSTALLOGRAPHICA INDEX SYSTEM
BNS COMPUTER ASSISTED INDEXING PROGRAM
BOOKDEX
GOLDEN RETRIEVER
INDEX EDITOR
INDEX PREPARATION SYSTEM
INFORONICS
LIBRARY MATE (PREVIOUSLY LIBRARIAN)
MACREX
METAMICRO
MICREX
MICRO CAIRS
MICRO INDEXING SYSTEM
MICROINDEX
MICROPSI
MIKRO POLYDOC
NEWSDEX
NOTA BENE
POPPYTIME INDEX BUILD SYSTEM
ROTHINES INDEXING AND ABSTRACTING SOFTWARE
TEQLIB

Information retrieval

AQUILA
ASSASSIN PC
ASSOCIATIVE FILE PROCESSOR
BOOKSHELF
BRS SEARCH
DATAFAX
DATAPATH
EAGLE
FACTFINDER
FINDER
FOCUS
GOLDEN RETRIEVER
I
INFOBASE
INFOKOM
INMAGIC BIBLIO
INMAGIC MICRO
INSTANTCOM 3.1
KWIRS
LIBRARIAN
LIBRARY MATE
LITER
MAGPIE
MASTER LEGAL SYSTEM PC
MICRO CAIRS
MICRO STATUS
MICROBIRD
MICROFILE
MIKRO POLYDOC
MIPS
MIRABILIS
NOTA BENE
NUTSHELL INFORMATION FILER 2.0
PERSONAL BIBLIOGRAPHIC SYSTEM
PINDOC
PLIDOS
POPPYTIME INFORMATION RETRIEVAL SYSTEM
PRO-CITE
PROFESSIONAL BIBLIOGRAPHIC SYSTEM 2.6
QUICK SEARCH LIBRARIAN
RASMUS
RECALL
REFLES : REFERENCE LIBRARIAN ENHANCEMENT SYSTEM
SCI MATE
SEEKEASY
SILICON OFFICE
SIR
SIRE
STAR
STRIX
TAMIL
TEQLIB
TESTMAGIC
TIN : THE INFORMATION NAVIGATOR

Information retrieval : commercial database subsets

BIO SUPERFILE
BITS
BITTERN
GPO LASERFILE (TM)
LIS
LSSI LASERFILE SYSTEM
MICRO SCAN : DISCLOSURE
MICRO SEARCH
PC ABSTRACTS ACCESS PAK
SCI-MATE
WILSONDISC

Interlibrary loans

ACCESS (TM) — MICROCOMPUTER NETWORK SYSTEM

AIM 2 — INTERLENDING SYSTEM
ARTTEL
F.I.L.L.S. : FAST INTERLIBRARY LOANS AND STATISTICS
F.I.L.L.S. : FAST INTERLIBRARY LOANS AND STATISTICS 2.0
ILL FORMS PRINTER
LIS
LOAN
OCLC ILL MICRO ENHANCER
ON TYME
VIDACCESS

Issue system

ADLIB 2
ALC BASIC LIBRARY SERIES
APPLE CIRC
BBC MICRO LIBRARY SYSTEM
BIBLIO LEND
BIBLIO TEL
BOOKSHELF
BOOKTRAK
BOOKTRAK I
BOOKWORM
CALM : COMPUTER AIDED LIBRARY MANAGEMENT
CARD DATALOG
CIRC
CIRCA I
CIRCA II
CIRCULATION MANAGEMENT SYSTEM
CIRCULATION MANAGER
CIRCULATION PLUS
DATA DUE
DYNIX
EASTWIND
HIGHSMITH CIRCULATION SYSTEM
I-CIRC
INFOQUEST
INMAGIC BIBLIO
INNOVACQ
INTEGRATED MICROCOMPUTER LIBRARY SYSTEM
KAMBIS
LASS
LENDING LIBRARY (THE)
LIBRAFILE
LIBRAFILE : BARCODE VERSION
LIBRARIAN
LIBRARY CIRCULATION MANAGER
LIBRARY CIRCULATION SYSTEM II
LIBRARY CIRCULATION SYSTEM III
LIBRARY MANAGEMENT SYSTEM
LIBS 100 : SYSTEM 23
LICON
LIS
MICROLIBRARY
NONESUCH CIRCULATION SYSTEM
OCELOT CIRCULATION MODULE
OCELOT LIBRARY SYSTEM
OFFICE MANAGER
ORCHARD SYSTEMS CIRCULATION MANAGEMENT SYSTEM
OVERDUE WRITER
OVERNIGHT WRITER
PEARL 4.0
SABINI
TAMIL
TELEPEN LIBRARY SYSTEM
TPS 400 ON-LINE INTERFACE
UNICORN COLLECTION MANAGEMENT SYSTEM

Labels

CALM 3.1 : CARD AND LABEL MANAGER
CARD CATALOG
CARDPRO : APPLE
CARDPRO : TRS
CATALOG CARD AND LABEL WRITER
CATALOG CARD MAKER III
MICROMARC
SPINE POCKET CARD LABELS PROGRAM
TELEMARC III
TPS 450 ON-LINE SPINE LABEL PRINTING SYSTEM
ULTRACARD

Law libraries

LASS
LAWTERM

Legal documentation

MASTER LEGAL SYSTEM PC
MIPS

Library guiding

BIBLIO GUIDE

Marc interface

OCELOT CATALOGUE MODULE
SC 350
TERM MARC

Marc record interface

BIB BASE MARC
LIBS 100 : SYSTEM 23

Medical libraries

MEDICAL LIBRARIAN
LIS

Online access to Alanet

DATALINK

Online access to BBC world reporter database

REPORTERM

Online access to Blaise-line

CORTEX

Online access to BRS

BIBLIO LINK
DATALINK
PRO SEARCH
PRO SEARCH 1.04
SCI MATE
SEARCH MASTER

Online access to CLSI

DATALINK

Online access to Cas Online

BASIL

Online access to DARC

BASIL

Online access to Data Star

BASIL

Online access to Dialog

BASIL
BIBLIO LINK
BOOKENDS TRANSLATORS
DATALINK
DIALOGLINK
DIALTERM
OLSAM : ONLINE SEARCH ASSISTANCE MACHINE
PRO SEARCH

PRO SEARCH 1.04
SCI MATE

Online access to Dimdi
BASIL

Online access to Disclosure
MICRODISCLOSURE

Online access to Dow Jones news retrieval
ASTRA FINANCIAL JOURNAL
SEARCH MASTER

Online access to DRI database
VISILINK

Online access to Easynet
DATALINK

Online access to ESA IRS Dialtech
ESATERM
MIKROTEL

Online access to Eurolex
LAWTERM

Online access to GCAM
BASIL

Online access to IAC
SEARCH HELPER

Online access to ISI
SCI MATE

Online access to Medlars
BIBLIO LINK

Online access to Medline
BASIL
BOOKENDS TRANSLATORS
SCI MATE
SEARCH MASTER

Online access to OCLC
BIBLIO LINK
LSTERM COMMUNICATIONS SOFTWARE

Online access to Questel 1
BASIL

Online access to Questel 2
BASIL

Online access to RLIN
BIBLIO LINK

Online access to SDC
BASIL
OLSAM : ONLINE SEARCH ASSISTANCE MACHINE
SEARCH MASTER

Online access to Telecom gold
GOLDTERM

Online access to Wilson
WILSEARCH

Online access to Wilsonline
DATALINK

Online search aid
ACSESS
ASCOM IV
ASSIST
BASIL
BOOKSHELF
CONNECT
COPYLINK
CORTEX
CROSSTALK
CROSSTALK XVI
DATABASE FINDING AID
DATALINK
DATAPATH
DIALOGLINK
DRM TELETYPE EMULATOR
HEADLINE
I & D SOFTWARE
INFOKOM
INSTANTCOM ESL
INSTANTCOM 3.1
INTEGRATED MICROCOMPUTER LIBRARY SYSTEM
IT : INFORMATION TRANSFER PROGRAM
LIAISON
MAGPIE
METAID
MIKROTEL
MITE
NIC SEARCH PACKAGE
ONLINE PRICING SIMULATOR
OLSAM : ONLINE SEARCH ASSISTANCE MACHINE
PC DIAL
PC NET LINK
PLIDOS
POST PLUS
POST PLUS BRIEFCASE
POST PLUS CONCURRENT
PRO SEARCH
PRO SEARCH 1.04
RASMUS
REVITEL
SEARCH MASTER
SMART TERMINAL
SMARTCOM II
SWIFT
TANDATA VIEWTEX MICROPACK
TTY
VICOM
WILSEARCH
XMODEM PC

Orders : online
INNOVACQ
LINX
PEARL 4.0

Overdue notices
ELEMENTARY OVERDUE COLLECTOR
ELEMENTARY OVERDUE WRITER

Overdues
LIBRARY HELPER OVERDUES
LIBRARY MICROTOOLS : OVERDUES
LIBRARY MONITOR
OVERDUE BOOKS
OVERDUE COLLECTOR

Reference management
BOOKENDS
BOOKENDS EXTENDED
BOOKENDS PRO DOS
LIBRAMATIX
LITER
PLIDOS

PULSAR
REFLES : REFERENCE LIBRARIAN ENHANCEMENT SYSTEM
SCI MATE EDITOR
SEARCHLIT
SEARCHLIT 2.0
TEQLIB
25.02

Reformatting

BIBLIO LINK
BOOKENDS TRANSLATORS
DATA TRANSFER SYSTEM
HEADFORM

Report generation

SILICON OFFICE

Retrospective conversion

LSSI LASERFILE SYSTEM
MICROCON
MICROLIBRARY
MICROMARC
MITINET RETRO
TERM MARC
TPS 400 ON-LINE INTERFACE
ULTRACARD MARC

School libraries

AV CATALOGUE WRITER
BOOKWORM
ELEMENTARY LIBRARY MEDIA SKILLS
INTEGRATED MICOCOMPUTER LIBRARY SYSTEM
KWIRS
LIBRAFILE
LIBRAFILE : BARCODE VERSION
LIBRARY CIRCULATION MANAGER
LIBRARY MICROTOOLS : OVERDUES
LIBRARY MONITOR
LIBRARY SKILLS
LIBRARY SKILLS : RIGHT ON
LIBRARY USAGE SKILLS
OVERDUE BOOKS
SIR

Serials control

ADLIB 2
ALC BASIC LIBRARY SERIES
BOOKSHELF
BOOKTRAK
CALM : COMPUTER AIDED LIBRARY MANAGEMENT
CARD DATALOG
CHECKMATE
CHECKMATE MTS
INMAGIC BIBLIO
INNOVACQ
KAMBIS
LIBRARY MANAGEMENT SYSTEM
LIDAS
LINX
LIS
LS2000 SERIALS CONTROL
METAMICRO
MICROCOMPUTERISED PERIODICAL MANAGEMENT SYSTEM
MICROLIBRARY
MICROLINX CHECK-IN
OCELOT LIBRARY SYSTEM
OCELOT SERIALS MODULE
PEARL 4.0
PERCS
PERIODICALS
SC 350
SERIALS MANAGEMENT SYSTEM : SMS
UNICORN COLLECTION MANAGEMENT SYSTEM
UNIVERSITY OF MINNESOTA PERIODICALS MANAGEMENT
ZEUS

Statistics

ASSOCIATIVE FILE PROCESSOR
CREATE
MICRO SCAN : DISCLOSURE
ONLINE PRICING SIMULATOR

Thesaurus control

ADLIB 2
ASSOCIATIVE FILE PROCESSOR
CALM : COMPUTER AIDED LIBRARY MANAGEMENT
LIBRARY MANAGEMENT SYSTEM
MICRO CAIRS
RASMUS
SABINI
SIRE
THESAURUS
TIN : THE INFORMATION NAVIGATOR

User education

BIBLIO GUIDE
CALICO
CALL NUMBER ORDER
ELEMENTARY LIBRARY MEDIA SKILLS
LIBRARY QUIZ
LIBRARY SEARCH AND SOLVE
LIBRARY SKILLS
LIBRARY SKILLS : RIGHT ON
LIBRARY USAGE SKILLS
MCGRAW HILL INTERACTIVE AUTHORING SYSTEM
PRIVATE TUTOR
TOP CLASS

Viewdata

ASSIST
METALOGUE

Viewdata : access to remote systems

ACCESS (TM) — MICROCOMPUTER NETWORK SYSTEM
PREDITOR
PRISM
PVS 990
REVITEL
TANDATA VIEWTEX MICROPACK
VICOM
VIDACCESS

Viewdata : inhouse systems

PREDITOR
PVS 990
TANDATA VIEWTEX MICROPACK

Word processing

ASSASSIN PC
BITS : BOEING INTELLIGENT TERMINAL SYSTEM
CORMORANT
FACTFINDER
HEADSET
I & D SOFTWARE
INDEX PREPARATION SYSTEM
INFOKOM
INSTANTCOM ESL
INSTANTCOM 3.1
LIS
METAMICRO
MIPS
NOTA BENE

PERSONAL BIBLIOGRAPHIC SYSTEM
POPPYTIME INDEX BUILD SYSTEM
POPPYTIME INFORMATION RETRIEVAL SYSTEM
POST PLUS
POST PLUS BRIEFCASE
POST PLUS CONCURRENT
SEARCHLIT 2.0
SILICON OFFICE

Act Apricot see Apricot

Alpha Micro 100
REFLES : REFERENCE LIBRARIAN ENHANCEMENT SYSTEM

Alpha Microsystems Business Computer
STAR

Altos (Model not specified)
BOOKSHELF
INFOBASE
SWIFT

Altos ACS 8000-10
FILM BOOKING

Apple (Model not specified)
BIBLIOGRAPHY COMPILER
COPYLINK
CTI
DATAFAX
LIBRARY SEARCH AND SOLVE
LIBRARY SKILLS
MICRO SEARCH
MICROMARC
ONLINE PRICING SIMULATOR

Apple II
A V EQUIPMENT INVENTORY
ACCESS (TM) — MICROCOMPUTER NETWORK SYSTEM
APPLE CIRC
ART PRINT INVENTORY
BOOKWORM
CALICO
CALL NUMBER ORDER
CATALOG CARD AND LABEL WRITER
DATA TRANSFER SYSTEM
DATABASE FINDING AID
EAGLE
KWIRS
LIBRARY ACCOUNTS
LIBRARY CIRCULATION MANAGER
LIBRARY MATE (PREVIOUSLY LIBRARIAN)
LIBRARY QUIZ
LIBRARY USAGE SKILLS
LOAN
MICROINDEX
ORCHARD SYSTEMS CIRCULATION MANAGEMENT SYSTEM
PERSONAL BIBLIOGRAPHIC SYSTEM
PRISM
QUICK SEARCH LIBRARIAN
SEARCH HELPER
SEARCH MASTER
TEQLIB
VIDACCESS

Apple II c
BOOKENDS EXTENDED
BOOKENDS PRO DOS
CALM 3.1: CARD AND LABEL MANAGER
CATALOG CARD MAKER III
EASTWIND
LIBRARY CIRCULATION SYSTEM II
LIBRARY HELPER OVERDUES
LIBRARY MATE (PREVIOUSLY LIBRARIAN)
PERSONAL BIBLIOGRAPHIC SYSTEM
VICOM

Apple II e
A V CATALOG WRITER
A V EQUIPMENT INVENTORY
A V INVENTORY
ACCESS (TM) — MICROCOMPUTER NETWORK SYSTEM
ACCESSION PLUS
ART PRINT INVENTORY
BOOKENDS
BOOKENDS EXTENDED
BOOKENDS PRO DOS
BOOKENDS TRANSLATORS
BOOKTRAK
BOOKTRAK I
CALM 3.1 : CARD AND LABEL MANAGER
CARDPREP
CARDPRO : APPLE
CATALOG CARD MAKER III
CATALOGIT
CIRCA I
CIRCULATION MANAGEMENT SYSTEM
CIRCULATION PLUS
COMPUTER CAT ; MULTI USER
CREATE
DATA TRANSFER SYSTEM
DATABASE FINDING AID
EASTWIND
ELEMENTARY LIBRARY MEDIA SKILLS
ELEMENTARY OVERDUE WRITER
FICTION FINDER
HIGHSMITH CIRCULATION SYSTEM
ILL FORMS PRINTER
INTEGRATED MICROCOMPUTER LIBRARY SYSTEM
LIBRARY CIRCULATION SYSTEM II
LIBRARY CIRCULATION SYSTEM III
LIBRARY HELPER OVERDUES
LIBRARY QUIZ
LIBRARY SKILLS : RIGHT ON
MEDIA AND EQUIPMENT MANAGEMENT
MICRO SEARCH
MICROBIRD
MICROCOMPUTERISED PERIODICAL MANAGEMENT SYSTEM
MICROFILE
MITINET RETRO
ORDERIT
OVERDUE BOOKS
PERSONAL BIBLIOGRAPHIC SYSTEM
SCI MATE
SEARCH HELPER
TELEMARC III
TPS 400 ON LINE INTERFACE
TPS 450 ON LINE SPINE LABEL PRINTING SYSTEM
VICOM
VIDACCESS

Apple II Plus
A V CATALOG WRITER
A V EQUIPMENT INVENTORY
A V INVENTORY
ACCESS (TM) — MICROCOMPUTER NETWORK SYSTEM
ACCESSION PLUS
ART PRINT INVENTORY
BIBLIOGRAPHY WRITER
BOOKENDS
BOOKENDS PRO DOS
BOOKENDS TRANSLATORS
BOOKTRAK
CALICO
CALM 3.1 : CARD AND LABEL MANAGER
CARDPREP
CARDPRO : APPLE
CATALOG CARD AND LABEL WRITER
CATALOGIT

CIRCULATION MANAGEMENT SYSTEM
CIRCULATION PLUS
CREATE
DATA TRANSFER SYSTEM
ELEMENTARY LIBRARY MEDIA SKILLS
ELEMENTARY OVERDUE COLLECTOR
ELEMENTARY OVERDUE WRITER
FICTION FINDER
ILL FORMS PRINTER
LIBRARY CIRCULATION SYSTEM II
LIBRARY HELPER OVERDUES
LIBRARY MATE (PREVIOUSLY LIBRARIAN)
LIBRARY MONITOR
LIBRARY QUIZ
LIBRARY SKILLS : RIGHT ON
MARS : MICROCOMPUTER ARCHIVES AND RECORDS MANAGEMENT SYSTEMS
MEDIA AND EQUIPMENT MANAGEMENT
MICRO SEARCH
MICROFILE
MITINET RETRO
ORDERIT
OVERDUE BOOKS
OVERDUE COLLECTOR
OVERDUE WRITER
OVERNIGHT WRITER
PERSONAL BIBLIOGRAPHIC SYSTEM
SCI MATE
SEARCH HELPER
TELEMARC III
VICOM
VIDACCESS

Apple III

APPLE CIRC
BOOKENDS
BOOKENDS TRANSLATORS
CIRCA I
CIRCA II
EASTWIND
HIGHSMITH CIRCULATION SYSTEM
ILL FORMS PRINTER
LIBRARY MATE (PREVIOUSLY LIBRARIAN)
PERSONAL BIBLIOGRAPHIC SYSTEM

Apple Macintosh

BIBLIO LINK
FACTFINDER
MITE
PROFESSIONAL BIBLIOGRAPHIC SYSTEM
SMARTCOM II

Apricot

ASSIST
CATALOGUE CARDS
CIRC
CURRENT TITLES SYSTEM
HEADLINE
HEADSET
I
I-CIRC
MICRO CAIRS
MIRABILIS
PERCS
RASMUS
RECALL
SILICON OFFICE

Atari

MEDIA AND EQUIPMENT MANAGEMENT

AT+T PC

INDEX PREPARATION SYSTEM

BBC (Model not specified)

DIALTERM
ESATERM
GOLDTERM
HEADLINE
LAWTERM
LIBRAFILE
LIBRAFILE : BARCODE VERSION
PRISM
PROTOKOL
REPORTERM
SWIFT

BBC Model B

BBC MICRO LIBRARY SYSTEM
PREDITOR

Bull Micral 30

PINDOC

Burroughs B 20

SEARCH MASTER

CAL PC

HEADLINE

CASU Mini

METAID

CASU Super C

METAID

CCP/M-86 (Operating system)

LIBRAMATIX
LIBRARIAN

Cifer

ASSIST
MIRABILIS

Cifer 18xx Series

HEADLINE

Cifer 2684

SWIFT

Cifer 28xx Series

HEADLINE

CLSI Terminal

DATALINK

Columbia PC

ASSIST
HEADLINE
SWIFT

Columbia MPC

MICROMARC

Comart

BIBLIO BUY
BIBLIO GUIDE
BIBLIO LEND
BIBLIO TEL
HEADLINE

Commodore (Model not specified)

OFFICE MANAGER

Commodore 64
- A V EQUIPMENT INVENTORY
- ACCESSION PLUS
- ART PRINT INVENTORY
- CATALOGIT
- DATE DUE
- LIBRARY SKILLS : RIGHT ON
- ORDERIT
- OVERDUE BOOKS

Commodore 2001
- DATE DUE

Commodore 4016
- DATE DUE

Commodore 4032
- DATE DUE

Commodore 8000 Series
- PERIODICALS

Commodore 8032
- BNS COMPUTER ASSISTED INDEXING PROGRAM
- DATE DUE
- PLIDOS
- POPPYTIME INFORMATION RETRIEVAL SYSTEM
- SILICON OFFICE

Commodore 8050
- PLIDOS

Commodore 8096
- SILICON OFFICE

Commodore Pet
- ACCESSION PLUS
- ARTTEL
- BIBLIOGRAPHY COMPILER
- BOOKWORM
- CATALOGIT
- LIBRARY BUDGET FTE CALC
- LIBRARY SKILLS : RIGHT ON
- MEDIA AND EQUIPMENT MANAGEMENT
- ORDERIT
- OVERDUE BOOKS
- PET COMPUTER LIBRARY CARD MAKER

Commodore Pet 8000 Series
- MICROINDEX

Compaq
- ASSIST
- DIALOGLINK
- HEADLINE

Concurrent dos (Operating system)
- LIBRARIAN

Control Data CD 110
- INFOBASE

CP/M (operating system)
- AQUILA
- BIO SUPERFILE
- BITS
- CARD DATALOG
- CONNECT
- HEADFORM
- INMAGIC BIBLIO
- INMAGIC MICRO
- MICREX
- MICROPSI
- MIKRO POLYDOC
- POST PLUS
- TANDATA VIEWTEX MICROPACK
- TTY

CP/M 2.0 (Operating system)
- SEEKEASY

CP/M 2.1 (Operating system)
- SEEKEASY

CP/M 2.2 (Operating system)
- MACREX
- ROTHINES INDEXING AND ABSTRACTING SOFTWARE
- SEEKEASY

CP/M 2.2+ (Operating system)
- SCOLAS

CP/M-80 (Operating system)
- THESAURUS

CP/M-86 (Operating system)
- HEADFORM
- INMAGIC BIBLIO
- INMAGIC MICRO
- LIBRAMATIX
- MIKRO POLYDOC
- TANDATA VIEWTEX MICROPACK
- TTY

Cromenco (Model not specified)
- SWIFT

Cromenco System Three
- HEADLINE

Crystal
- BOOKSHELF

Data General Micros
- EASTWIND

Datapoint Dos (Operating system)
- LASS

DEC II/23 Series
- LIBS 100 : SYSTEM 23
- LIS

DEC II/73 Series
- LIS

DEC Micro PDP II/23
- ASSOCIATIVE FILE PROCESSOR
- MICROBIRD

DEC PDP 11
- MICROBIRD

DEC Personal Computers
- SILICON OFFICE

DEC Professional
- PEARL 4.0

DEC Rainbow
ASSIST
EAGLE
HEADLINE
HEADSET
INFOBASE
RECALL
SMARTCOM II

Eagle II E
SEARCH HELPER

Eagle Systems
MICRO CAIRS

Epson HX-20
CIRC

Epson PX 8
POST PLUS BRIEFCASE

Fortune
OFFICE MANAGER
TAMIL

Fortune 32:16
MICRO STATUS

Franklin Ace
TELEMARC III

Franklin Ace 1000
MICRO SEARCH

Future Technology
MICRO CAIRS

GA
BOOKSHELF

General Automation see GA

HP 150
HEADLINE
HEADSET
MICRO CAIRS
SMARTCOM II

IBM PC
25 : 02
ACCESSION PLUS
AIM 2 — INTERLENDING SYSTEM
ASCOM IV
ASSASSIN PC
ASSIST
BIB BASE
BIB BASE ACQ
BIB BASE ACQ AND BIB BASE CAT COMBINED
BIB BASE CAT
BIB BASE MARC
BIB BASE TEXT
BIBLIO LINK
BITS : BOEING INTELLIGENT TERMINAL SYSTEM
BOOKDEX
BOOKENDS
CALM 3.1 : CARD AND LABEL MANAGER
CATALOG CARD PROGRAM
CATALOGIT
CATALOGUE CARDS
CHECKMATE
CIRCA II
COPYLINK
CROSSTALK
CURRENT TITLES SYSTEM
DATA TRANSFER SYSTEM
DATABASE FINDING AID
DATAFAX
DATAPATH
DIALOGLINK
EAGLE
F.I.L.L.S.: FAST INTERLIBRARY LOANS AND STATISTICS
F.I.L.L.S.: FAST INTERLIBRARY LOANS AND STATISTICS 2.0
FINDER
GOLDEN RETRIEVER
GPO LASERFILE (TM)
HEADLINE
HEADSET
I & D SOFTWARE
INDEX EDITOR
INDEX PREPARATION SYSTEM
INFOBASE
INFOKOM
INFOQUEST
INSTANTCOM 3.1
INSTANTCOM ESL
KAMBIS
LIAISON
LS2000 SERIALS CONTROL
LSSI LASERFILE SYSTEM
LSTERM COMMUNICATIONS SOFTWARE
McGRAW HILL INTERACTIVE AUTHORING SYSTEM
METALOGUE
MICRO CAIRS
MICRO INDEXING SYSTEM
MICRO SCAN : DISCLOSURE
MICROBIRD
MICRODISCLOSURE
MICROLINX CHECK-IN
MICROMARC
MIKROTEL
MIRABILIS
MITINET RETRO
NEWSDEX
NONESUCH ACQUISITIONS SYSTEM
NONESUCH CIRCULATION SYSTEM
NUTSHELL INFORMATION FILER 2.0
OCELOT ACQUISITIONS MODULE
OCELOT CATALOGUE MODULE
OCELOT CIRCULATION MODULE
OCELOT LIBRARY SYSTEM
OCELOT SERIALS MODULE
OCLC ILL MICRO ENHANCER
OFFICE MANAGER
ONLINE PRICING SIMULATOR
ORDERIT
ORICAT
OVERDUE BOOKS
PC ABSTRACTS ACCESS PAK
PC DIAL
PERCS
POPPYTIME INDEX BUILD SYSTEM
POST PLUS CONCURRENT
PRISM
PRIVATE TUTOR
PRO-CITE
PRO SEARCH
PRO SEARCH 1.04
RASMUS
RECALL
REVITEL
SC 350
SCI MATE
SCI MATE EDITOR
SEARCH HELPER
SEARCH MASTER

SEARCHLIT
SEARCHLIT 2.0
SERIALS MANAGEMENT SYSTEM : SMS
SILICON OFFICE
SIRE
SMARTCOM II
SWIFT
TEQLIB
TERM MARC
TIN : THE INFORMATION NAVIGATOR
TOP CLASS
ULTRACARD
ULTRACARD MARC
WILSEARCH
XMODEM PC

IBM PC AT

ALC BASIC LIBRARY SERIES
ASCOM IV
ASSASSIN PC
BIB BASE ACQ AND BIB BASE CAT COMBINED
BIB BASE CAT
BIB BASE MARC
BIB BASE TEXT
BIBLIO LINK
CALM : COMPUTER AIDED LIBRARY MANAGEMENT
CATALOGUE CARDS
CURRENT TITLES SYSTEM
DIALOGLINK
F.I.L.L.S.: FAST INTERLIBRARY LOANS AND STATISTICS
F.I.L.L.S.: FAST INTERLIBRARY LOANS AND STATISTICS 2.0
HEADLINE
HEADSET
INFOQUEST
KAMBIS
LICON
MICROLIBRARY
MIRABILIS
NUTSHELL INFORMATION FILER 2.0
OCELOT ACQUISITIONS MODULE
OCELOT CATALOGUE MODULE
OCELOT CIRCULATION MODULE
OCELOT LIBRARY SYSTEM
OCELOT SERIALS MODULE
PC NET LINK
PERCS
PINDOC
PRO-CITE
PRO SEARCH
PRO SEARCH 1.04
RECALL
SABINI
SCI MATE EDITOR
TERM MARC
ULTRACARD MARC
WILSEARCH

IBM PC Compatibles

AIM2 — INTERLENDING SYSTEM
ASCOM IV
ASSASSIN PC
ASSIST
BIB BASE MARC
BIBLIO LINK
CALM 3.1 : CARD AND LABEL MANAGER
CALM : COMPUTER AIDED LIBRARY MANAGEMENT
CATALOG CARD PROGRAM
CATALOGUE CARDS
COPYLINK
CROSSTALK
DATAFAX
DIALOGLINK
GPO LASERFILE (TM)
I & D SOFTWARE
INDEX PREPARATION SYSTEM
INSTANTCOM 3.1
INSTANTCOM ESL
LICON
MICROLIBRARY
NONESUCH ACQUISITIONS SYSTEM
NONESUCH CIRCULATION SYSTEM
NOTA BENE
NUTSHELL INFORMATION FILER 2.0
OCELOT ACQUISITIONS MODULE
OCELOT CATALOGUE MODULE
OCELOT CIRCULATION MODULE
OCELOT LIBRARY SYSTEM
OCELOT SERIALS MODULE
PC ABSTRACTS ACCESS PAK
PERCS
PINDOC
POST PLUS CONCURRENT
PRO-CITE
PRO SEARCH
PRO SEARCH 1.04
RASMUS
RECALL
SABINI
SCI MATE EDITOR
SEARCH MASTER
SEARCHLIT 2.0
SERIALS MANAGEMENT SYSTEM : SMS
SMARTCOM II
TIN : THE INFORMATION NAVIGATOR
TOP CLASS
WILSEARCH
XMODEM PC

IBM PC XT

ALC BASIC LIBRARY SERIES
ASCOM IV
ASSASSIN PC
BIB BASE ACQ
BIB BASE ACQ AND BIB BASE CAT COMBINED
BIB BASE CAT
BIB BASE MARC
BIB BASE TEXT
BIBLIO LINK
BOOKDEX
CALM : COMPUTER AIDED LIBRARY MANAGEMENT
CATALOGUE CARDS
CHECKMATE
CIRCA I
CIRCA II
CURRENT TITLES SYSTEM
DIALOGLINK
EASTWIND
F.I.L.L.S.: FAST INTERLIBRARY LOANS AND STATISTICS
F.I.L.L.S.: FAST INTERLIBRARY LOANS AND STATISTICS 2.0
FINDER
GOLDEN RETRIEVER
HEADLINE
HEADSET
INDEX PREPARATION SYSTEM
INSTANTCOM 3.1
INSTANTCOM ESL
IT : INFORMATION TRANSFER PROGRAM
KAMBIS
LICON
MAGPIE
MASTER LEGAL SYSTEM PC
MICRO INDEXING SYSTEM
MICRO SCAN : DISCLOSURE
MICRO STATUS

MICRODISCLOSURE
MICROLIBRARY
MIKROTEL
MIRABILIS
NEWSDEX
NUTSHELL INFORMATION FILER 2.0
OCELOT ACQUISITIONS MODULE
OCELOT CATALOGUE MODULE
OCELOT CIRCULATION MODULE
OCELOT LIBRARY SYSTEM
OCELOT SERIALS MODULE
OCLC ILL MICRO ENHANCER
PC DIAL
PC NET LINK
PERCS
PINDOC
PRO-CITE
PRO SEARCH
PRO SEARCH 1.04
RECALL
SABINI
SCI MATE
SCI MATE EDITOR
SEARCH HELPER
SILICON OFFICE
SIRE
TEQLIB
TERM MARC
TOP CLASS
ULTRACARD
ULTRACARD MARC
WILSEARCH
WILSONDISC

ICL PC
MEDICAL LIBRARIAN

ICL DRS 20
ACSESS
FOCUS

Infoshare (Novell) (Operating system)
LIBRARY MANAGEMENT SYSTEM

Innovacq Multi Processor Computer
INNOVACQ

Intel ITPS 86 445
MIPS

Kaypro 4
SCI MATE

Kaypro 10
SCI MATE

Logabax Personna 1600
PINDOC

MP/M (Operating System)
CARD DATALOG
MIKRO POLYDOC

MP/M 86
MIKRO POLYDOC

MS DOS (Operating system)
ACQUEST
BIO SUPERFILE
BITS
CARD DATALOG
CONNECT
HEADFORM
INMAGIC BIBLIO
INMAGIC MICRO
LENDING LIBRARY (THE)
LIBRAMATIX
LIBRARY MANAGEMENT SYSTEM
MIKRO POLYDOC
POST PLUS
TANDATA VIEWTEX MICROPACK
THESAURUS
TTY

MS DOS 2.0+ (Operating system)
MACREX

NCT Tower
TAMIL

North Star
OLSAM : ONLINE SEARCH ASSISTANCE MACHINE

Oasis (Operating System)
ACTA CRYSTALLOGRAPHICA INDEX SYSTEM

OCLC M300 Workstation
F.I.L.L.S.: FAST INTERLIBRARY LOANS AND STATISTICS
F.I.L.L.S.: FAST INTERLIBRARY LOANS AND STATISTICS 2.0
GPO LASERFILE (TM)
LS2000 SERIALS CONTROL
LSTERM COMMUNICATIONS SOFTWARE
SC 350

Olivetti M21
HEADLINE

Olivetti M24
HEADLINE
LIAISON
OPAC ACCESS
PINDOC

Onyx
MICROBIRD

Onyx C 8002
TAMIL

Orion
METALOGUE

PC 750
I & D SOFTWARE

PC DOS (Operating System)
ACQUEST
CONNECT
INMAGIC BIBLIO
INMAGIC MICRO
LIBRAMATIX
THESAURUS

PC DOS 2.1+ (Operating system)
TANDATA VIEWTEX MICROPACK

PICK (Operating system)
DYNIX

Plexus
MICROBIRD
TAMIL

Rair
INFOBASE
MIRABILIS

Rediffusion Teleputer
EAGLE

Research Machines 380Z
SIR

Research Machines 480Z
SIR

Sage IV
MICROBIRD

Shelton SIG/NET
HEADLINE

Siemens
I & D SOFTWARE

Sirius
ASSIST
CATALOGUE CARDS
CORTEX
CURRENT TITLES SYSTEM
DRM TELETYPE EMULATOR
EAGLE
HEADLINE
HEADSET
I
I-CIRC
INFOBASE
LIBRARY ACCOUNTS
METALOGUE
MICRO CAIRS
MICROBIRD
MIRABILIS
OFFICE MANAGER
PERCS
POPPYTIME INDEX BUILD SYSTEM
PRISM
RASMUS
SILICON OFFICE
SWIFT

Sperry PC
HEADLINE

Superbrain
ASSIST
CURRENT TITLES SYSTEM
HEADLINE
INFOBASE
IT : INFORMATION TRANSFER PROGRAM
MIRABILIS
ORICAT
SWIFT

SWTPC S09
STRIX

SWTP S Plus
METAMICRO

Tandon PCX20
VIDEO LIBRARY SYSTEM

Tandy 1000
CATALOG CARD PROGRAM

Telepen System 4
TELEPEN LIBRARY SYSTEM

Televideo
INFOBASE

Televideo PM16
CALM : COMPUTER AIDED LIBRARY MANAGEMENT

Terak
UNIVERSITY OF MINNESOTA PERIODICALS MANAGEMENT

Texas Instruments (model not specified)
MICRO CAIRS

Texas Instruments DS900 Range
PVS 990

Texas Instruments Professional Computers
PRO SEARCH

Texas Instruments TX700
ARTTEL

Thompson Micromega 32
TAMIL

Thompson Micromega 160
PINDOC

TI Professional
CROSSTALK
INDEX EDITOR
SMARTCOM II

Torch
INFOBASE

Torch C500
HEADLINE

TRS
ONLINE PRICING SIMULATOR

TRS 80 (Model not specified)
ACCESSION PLUS
BIBLIOGRAPHY COMPILER
BOOKWORM
CARD
CATALOGIT
ORDERIT
OVERDUE BOOKS

TRS 80 Model I
A V EQUIPMENT INVENTORY
ART PRINT INVENTORY
LIBRARY QUIZ
SMART TERMINAL

TRS 80 Model II
BOOKDEX
BORROWERS FILE

CARD CATALOG
CARDPRO : TRS
ELEMENTARY OVERDUE WRITER
FINDER
GOLDEN RETRIEVER
INDEXING
LIBRARY CIRCULATION MANAGER
NEWSDEX
PULSAR
SCI MATE
SMART TERMINAL
SURVEYS
TEQLIB

TRS 80 Model III
A V CATALOG WRITER
A V EQUIPMENT INVENTORY
ART PRINT INVENTORY
AV CARD DIRECTORY PROGRAM
BIBLIOGRAPHY WRITER
CARDPREP
CARDPRO : TRS
CATALOG CARD AND LABEL WRITER
CATALOG CARD PROGRAM
CIRCULATION PLUS
ELEMENTARY OVERDUE COLLECTOR
LIBRARY CIRCULATION MANAGER
LIBRARY QUIZ
MEDIA AND EQUIPMENT MANAGEMENT
OVERDUE COLLECTOR
OVERDUE WRITER
OVERNIGHT WRITER
SMART TERMINAL
SPINE POCKET CARD LABELS PROGRAM

TRS 80 Model IV
A V EQUIPMENT INVENTORY
ART PRINT INVENTORY
AV CARD DIRECTORY PROGRAM
CARDPREP
CATALOG CARD PROGRAM
CIRCULATION PLUS
ELEMENTARY OVERDUE WRITER
LIBRARY QUIZ
MEDIA AND EQUIPMENT MANAGEMENT
SMART TERMINAL
SPINE POCKET CARD LABELS PROGRAM

TRS 80 Model IVD
AV CARD DIRECTORY PROGRAM
CATALOG CARD PROGRAM

TRS 80 Model IVP
AV CARD DIRECTORY PROGRAM
CATALOG CARD PROGRAM

TRS 80 Model 12
CARDPRO : TRS
FINDER
GOLDEN RETRIEVER
SCI MATE
SMART TERMINAL

TRS 100 Portable
N I C SEARCH PACKAGE

TRS Dos (Operating system)
POST PLUS

U/750
IT : INFORMATION TRANSFER PROGRAM

U/780
IT : INFORMATION TRANSFER PROGRAM

Unix (Operating system)
ADLIB2
BRS SEARCH
LENDING LIBRARY
UNICORN COLLECTION MANAGEMENT SYSTEM

Unixsys
TAMIL

Vax
IT : INFORMATION TRANSFER PROGRAM

Vector 3
SCI MATE

Vector 4
SCI MATE

Victor
PINDOC

Victor 9000
CORTEX
CROSSTALK
DATA TRANSFER SYSTEM
HEADLINE
HEADSET
SILICON OFFICE

Wang Office Information System (OIS 140)
ZEUS

Wang PC
CROSSTALK
NONESUCH ACQUISITIONS SYSTEM
NONESUCH CIRCULATION SYSTEM

Wang Professional
SMARTCOM II

Wang 2200C
LITER

Wicat MCS (Operating system)
LASS

Wordplex PC
HEADLINE

Xenix (Operating system)
BRS SEARCH

Xerox 820
POPPYTIME INDEX BUILD SYSTEM

Zenith PC
HEADLINE

Zenith Z100
BIB BASE
BIB BASE ACQ
ULTRACARD

Zenith Z110

BIB BASE ACQ
BIB BASE ACQ AND BIB BASE CAT COMBINED
BIB BASE CAT

Zenith Z120

BIB BASE ACQ
BIB BASE ACQ AND BIB BASE CAT COMBINED
BIB BASE CAT

ACI Computer Services
OCELOT ACQUISITIONS MODULE
OCELOT CATALOGUE MODULE
OCELOT CIRCULATION MODULE
OCELOT LIBRARY SYSTEM
OCELOT SERIALS MODULE

ADP Network Services
DATAPATH

AERE Harwell
MICRO STATUS

A.M. Computer Technology Ltd
VICOM

Aaron Smith Associates Inc
FINDER

Aball Software Inc
OCELOT ACQUISITIONS MODULE
OCELOT CATALOGUE MODULE
OCELOT CIRCULATION MODULE
OCELOT LIBRARY SYSTEM
OCELOT SERIALS MODULE

Acta Crystallographica
ACTA CRYSTALLOGRAPHICA INDEX SYSTEM

Adler, Elhanan see Elhanan Adler

Advanced Library Concepts Inc
ALC BASIC LIBRARY SERIES

Alert Cconsultants DFA
DATABASE FINDING AID

All Easy Corporation, Vertical Software Division
DATAFAX

Avery International Research Centre
MICROCOMPUTERISED PERIODICAL MANAGEMENT SYSTEM

BRS Europe
BRS SEARCH

BRS Software Products
BRS SEARCH

BVR Vedder
XMODEM PC

Bayside Indexing Service
MACREX

Biblio Tech Ltd
BIBLIO BUY
BIBLIO GUIDE
BIBLIO LEND
BIBLIO TEL
DYNIX

Blackwell Library Systems Inc
PEARL 4.0

Blackwell Technical Services Ltd
PEARL 4.0

Blumstein, Herbert
BOOKENDS
BOOKENDS TRANSLATORS

Boeing Computer Services (Europe) Ltd
BITS : BOEING INTELLIGENT TERMINAL SYSTEM

Bristol Software Factory Ltd
SILICON OFFICE

British Library Bibliographic Services
CORTEX

Brown, William L
DATE DUE

CLSI Ltd (UK) see also CLSI Inc (USA)
DATALINK
LIBS 100: SYSTEM 23
PEARL 4.0

CLSI Inc (USA) see also CLSI Ltd (UK)
DATALINK
LIBS 100: SYSTEM 23
PEARL 4.0

CTL Library Systems
APPLE CIRC

CALICO Inc *see* Computer Assisted Library Instruction Co Inc

Calvert, AH and DME
MACREX
MICREX

Cambridge Software Ltd
RASMUS

Capital Systems Group Inc
BOOKDEX
CARD
CHECKMATE
GOLDEN RETRIEVER
NEWSDEX
SCI MATE
ULTRACARD

CAPTEC, Computer Applied Techniques Ltd
LIAISON

Central Information Service, University of London
ACQUEST
CATALOGUE CARDS
CURRENT TITLES SYSTEM
MIRABILIS
PERCS

Central Management Library FAO Stephen Hume
LIDAS

Chemdata SA
TEXTO

Citech Ltd
SCI MATE

Class
CHECKMATE
CHECKMATE MTS
GOLDEN RETRIEVER
ON TYME
PRO SEARCH

Clinton-Essex-Franklin Library System
CARDPRO : APPLE

College of Librarianship Wales, FAO Mr R.F. Guy
MICROPSI

Colorado Computer West
LIBRARY MONITOR

Commbase Inc
ELEMENTARY LIBRARY MEDIA SKILLS

Compugramma Inc (Erica Mugglestone)
MICRO INDEXING SYSTEM

Computer Assisted Library Instruction Co Inc
CALICO
CALL NUMBER ORDER
FICTION FINDER

Computer Library Services International see CLSI

Computer Management Associates (Nathan Roseman)
BNS COMPUTER ASSISTED INDEXING PROGRAM

Computer Translation Inc
CTI

Computerland Stores
LOAN

Correlation Systems
SEEKEASY

Counting House Programs c/o James Thompson
PERIODICALS

Craig, Mr.
BORROWERS FILE
CARD CATALOG
INDEXING
SURVEYS

Cristad
BASIL

Ctrl. Alt. Deli.
TOP CLASS

Cuadra Associates Inc
STAR

D and H Software (USA)
A V INVENTORY

DTI Data Trek Inc
CARD DATALOG

Data Retrieval Corporation of America
MIPS

Databasix
ADLIB2

Datafusion Corp
ASSOCIATIVE FILE PROCESSOR

Dialog Information Services Inc
DIALOGLINK

Disclosure
MICRO SCAN : DISCLOSURE
MICRODISCLOSURE

Dynamic Microprocessor Associates
ASCOM IV

Dynix (UK) Ltd
DYNIX

East Tennessee State University c/o R.M. Kesner
MARS : MICROCOMPUTER ARCHIVES AND RECORDS MANAGEMENT SYSTEMS

Edinburgh University Library
LIBRARY ACCOUNTS

Educational Activities Inc
MEDIA AND EQUIPMENT MANAGEMENT

Elhanan Adler
ORICAT

Equinox Computers
LIBRARIAN

ERIC Clearinghouse on Information Resources
MICRO SEARCH

Eurotec Consultants Ltd
LIBRARIAN

FYI Inc
PC ABSTRACTS ACCESS PAK

Fachinformations Zentrum Technik E. V.
PLIDOS

Farestead Associates
MICROINDEX

Faxon
LINX
MICROLINX CHECK IN

Faxon Europe
LINX
MICROLINX CHECK-IN

Follett Software Company
A V CATALOG WRITER
BIBLIOGRAPHY WRITER
CARDPREP
CIRCULATION PLUS
ELEMENTARY OVERDUE COLLECTOR
ELEMENTARY OVERDUE WRITER
OVERDUE COLLECTOR
OVERDUE WRITER
OVERNIGHT WRITER

Ford & Co (South Shields) Ltd
FOCUS

Forethought Inc
FACTFINDER

Foxon-Maddocks Associates
INDEX PREPARATION SYSTEM

Franklin Research Center
OLSAM: ONLINE SEARCH ASSISTANCE MACHINE

G & G Software Ltd
BBC MICRO LIBRARY SYSTEM
LENDING LIBRARY (THE)

Gaylord Bros Inc
TELEMARC III

Genesys GMBH
I & D SOFTWARE

Geoglobal Systems Inc
LIBRARY MATE (PREVIOUSLY LIBRARIAN)

Georgetown University Medical Center
LIS

Graham Wheater & Son Ltd
LICON

H. W. Bookservice
LIBRAFILE
LIBRAFILE : BARCODE VERSION
PROTOKOL

H. W. Wilson Software Company
WILSEARCH
WILSONDISC

Hammett Microcomputer Division
BOOKWORM

"Hands On" Microcomputer Learning Centre
NOTA BENE

Harley M. Templeton
INDEX EDITOR

Hayes Microcomputer Products Inc
SMARTCOM II

Head Computers Ltd
HEADFORM
HEADLINE
HEADSET
INMAGIC BIBLIO
INMAGIC MICRO
TESTMAGIC

Heyden Datasystems
MICROFILE

Highsmith Co Inc
CIRCA I
HIGHSMITH CIRCULATION SYSTEM

Horemans, John
PET COMPUTER LIBRARY CARD MAKER

Howe Software
SMART TERMINAL

Howson Algraphy
DRM TELETYPE EMULATOR

IRS Dialtech
MIKROTEL

Informatics General Corporation
PC NET LINK

Information Access Co Inc, FAO Blowden Tarter
SEARCH HELPER

Information Inc
INFORONICS

Information Intelligence Inc
ACCESS(TM) MICROCOMPUTER
NETWORK SYSTEM
VIDACCESS

Information Management Consultants Ltd
PREDITOR

Information Management and Engineering Ltd
TIN : THE INFORMATION NAVIGATOR

Information Services, Control Data Ltd
INFOBASE

Information Solutions Inc
25:02

Information Systems Design
CIRC
I
I-CIRC

Information Transform Inc, FAO Hank Epstein
MITINET RETRO

Information und Kommunikation, FAO Dietrich Reith
INFOKOM
MASTER LEGAL SYSTEM PC

Informationsberatung
TIN:THE INFORMATION NAVIGATOR

Informazione Facile
TIN:THE INFORMATION NAVIGATOR

Inmagic Inc
INMAGIC MICRO

Innovative Interfaces Inc
INNOVACQ

Insoft Ltd
RECALL

Instantcom Xworld
INSTANTCOM 3.1
INSTANTCOM ESL

Institute for Scientific Information (UK)
SCI MATE
SCI MATE EDITOR

Institute for Scientific Information (USA)
SCI MATE
SCI MATE EDITOR

Interactive Microware
QUICK SEARCH LIBRARIAN

International Coffee Organisation
ACSESS

JMC Service Inc
LIBRARY USAGE SKILLS

K 12 Micromedia Publishing
CATALOG CARD AND LABEL WRITER
LIBRARY CIRCULATION MANAGER
LIBRARY MICROTOOLS: OVERDUES
LIBRARY SEARCH AND SOLVE
LIBRARY SKILLS

Karmac B.V.
KAMBIS

Kent Barlow Information Associates
AQUILA
BITTERN
CORMORANT
EAGLE
MAGPIE
STRIX
SWIFT

King County Library
FILM BOOKING

Leading Edge Software Products
NUTSHELL INFORMATION FILER 2.0

Learned Information (Europe) Ltd
CONNECT

Leatherhead Food Research Association
MICRO CAIRS

Legal Technology Group
DIALTERM
ESATERM
GOLDTERM
LAWTERM
REPORTERM

Leicester Polytechnic Library
AIM2 — INTERLENDING SYSTEM
ARTTEL
LIBRARY BUDGET FTE CALC
OPAC ACCESS

Libraries and Learning Inc
BIBLIOGRAPHY COMPILER

Library Processes System
AV CARD DIRECTORY PROGRAM
CATALOG CARD PROGRAM
SPINE POCKET CARD LABELS PROGRAM

Library Systems and Services Inc (A Gaylord Company)
GPO LASERFILE (TM)
LSSI LASERFILE SYSTEM
MICROMARC

Licon Systems
LICON

Litindex Inc
PULSAR

Logical Choice Computer Services Ltd
BOOKSHELF

London University, Central Information Service see Central Information Service, University of London

Lothlorien Software
INTEGRATED MICROCOMPUTER LIBRARY SYSTEM

MCTEL
POST PLUS
POST PLUS BRIEFCASE
POST PLUS CONCURRENT

MGS Computing Services
ASSASSIN PC
PVS 990

MSC Computers
CIRCA II

MVA Systematica
TTY

Mack Memorial Health Sciences Library
ILL FORMS PRINTER

Macneal Hospital, Finance Department/F.I.L.L.S.
F.I.L.L.S.: FAST INTERLIBRARY LOANS AND STATISTICS
F.I.L.L.S.: FAST INTERLIBRARY LOANS AND STATISTICS 2.0

Mars Group Services see MGS Computing Services

Master Data Center Inc
MASTER LEGAL SYSTEM PC

McGraw Hill Book Company
MCGRAW HILL INTERACTIVE AUTHORING SYSTEM

Mead Data Central
CROSSTALK XVI

Media Center Factory
A V EQUIPMENT INVENTORY
ART PRINT INVENTORY
LIBRARY QUIZ

Medisoft
SEARCHLIT
SEARCHLIT 2.0

Metamicro Library Systems Inc
METAMICRO

Metascybe Systems Ltd
METAID

Microdex
CREATE

Micromedia Ltd
DIALOGLINK
PRO SEARCH

Microsolutions
CIRCULATION MANAGER

Microstuf Inc
CROSSTALK
CROSSTALK XVI

Missing Link Computers Ltd
OFFICE MANAGER

Mycroft Labs Inc
MITE

NEC Information Systems
ASTRA FINANCIAL JOURNAL

Norsk Senter for Informatikk A S: Norwegian Centre for Informatics
MIKRO POLYDOC

OCLC
LS2000 SERIALS CONTROL
LSTERM COMMUNICATIONS SOFTWARE
MICROCON
OCLC ILL MICRO ENHANCER
SC 350

OCLC Europe
LS2000 SERIALS CONTROL
LSTERM COMMUNICATIONS SOFTWARE
MICROCON
OCLC ILL MICRO ENHANCER
SC 350

Online Simulations Inc
ONLINE PRICING SIMULATOR

Orchard Systems
CIRCULATION MANAGEMENT SYSTEM
ORCHARD SYSTEMS CIRCULATION MANAGEMENT SYSTEM

Organizacion de Consultores, SA
SABINI

Oriel Computer Services Ltd (Chipping Norton)
METALOGUE
OCELOT ACQUISITIONS MODULE
OCELOT CATALOGUE MODULE
OCELOT CIRCULATION MODULE
OCELOT LIBRARY SYSTEM
OCELOT SERIALS MODULE

Oriel Computers (Amsterdam)
METALOGUE
OCELOT ACQUISITIONS MODULE
OCELOT CATALOGUE MODULE
OCELOT CIRCULATION MODULE
OCELOT LIBRARY SYSTEM
OCELOT SERIALS MODULE

Oxford University Press
NOTA BENE

P & P Micro Distributors Ltd
FACTFINDER

Paton, Norman
KWIRS

Personal Bibliographic Software Inc
BIBLIO LINK
DATA TRANSFER SYSTEM
PC DIAL
PERSONAL BIBLIOGRAPHIC SYSTEM
PRO-CITE
PRO SEARCH 1.04
PROFESSIONAL BIBLIOGRAPHIC SYSTEM 2.6

Pinpoint Analysis Ltd
PINDOC

Poppytime Ltd
POPPYTIME INDEX BUILD SYSTEM
POPPYTIME INFORMATION RETRIEVAL SYSTEM

Pragmatix Pty Ltd
LIBRAMATIX

Prism Micro Products Ltd
PRISM

Pyramid Computer Systems Ltd
CALM : COMPUTER AIDED LIBRARY MANAGEMENT
FINDER
THESAURUS

RTZ Computer Services
MICRO CAIRS

Remidex Office Automation BV
REVITEL

Research Machines Ltd
SIR

Richmond Software Corporation
BOOKTRAK
BOOKTRAK I

Right On Programs
ACCESSION PLUS
CATALOGIT
LIBRARY SKILLS : RIGHT ON
ORDERIT
OVERDUE BOOKS

Ringgold Management Systems
NONESUCH ACQUISITIONS SYSTEM
NONESUCH CIRCULATION SYSTEM

Rothines Associates
ROTHINES INDEXING AND ABSTRACTING SOFTWARE

S B Electronic Systems Ltd
TELEPEN LIBRARY SYSTEM

SDC Information Services
SEARCH MASTER

Sashalom Pty Ltd
LASS

Sensible Software Inc
BOOKENDS
BOOKENDS EXTENDED
BOOKENDS PRO DOS
BOOKENDS TRANSLATED

Serials Management Services Ltd
SERIALS MANAGEMENT SYSTEM: SMS

Sirsi Corporation
UNICORN COLLECTION MANAGEMENT SYSTEM

Small Library Computing
BIB BASE
BIB BASE ACQ
BIB BASE ACQ AND BIB BASE CAT COMBINED
BIB BASE CAT
BIB BASE MARC
BIB BASE TEXT
SCOLAS
TERM MARC
ULTRACARD
ULTRACARD MARC

Software Consulting Services
SIRE
TEQLIB

Southern Micro Systems
LIBRARY HELPER OVERDUES

Speak Softly Inc
CALM 3.1: CARD AND LABEL MANAGER

Specialist Computer Systems and Software Ltd
BOOKSHELF

Starke, Hugh
CARDPRO: TRS

Stitchting N I C FAO Hans Van Nieuwkerk
N I C SEARCH PACKAGE

Sydney Dataproducts Inc
MICROLIBRARY

Sydney Development Corp
MICROLIBRARY

Sydney Library Products
MICROLIBRARY

TPS Electronics
TPS 400 ON-LINE INTERFACE
TPS 450 ON-LINE SPINE LABEL PRINTING SYSTEM

Tamil
TAMIL

Tandata Marketing Ltd
CROSSTALK
TANDATA VIEWTEX MICROPACK

Technology and Law Ltd, FAO Carolyn Hayman
MICROBIRD

Tescor Inc
OCELOT ACQUISITIONS MODULE
OCELOT CATALOGUE MODULE
OCELOT CIRCULATION MODULE
OCELOT LIBRARY SYSTEM
OCELOT SERIALS MODULE

Thomas, Dr. Karl
ZEUS

Thompson Henry Ltd
BIO SUPERFILE
BITS

Top Systems Ltd, Benny Segal
LIBRARY MANAGEMENT SYSTEM

USDA SEA, FAO John D Ross
LITER

US Digital Corp
COPYLINK

University of California, Graduate School of Library and Information Science
REFLES : REFERENCE LIBRARY ENHANCEMENT SYSTEM

University of London, Central Information Service see Central Information Service, University of London

University of Minnesota
UNIVERSITY OF MINNESOTA PERIODICALS MANAGEMENT

Userlink Communications Ltd
ASSIST
IT : INFORMATION TRANSFER PROGRAM

Utlas Corp
INFOQUEST
INNOVACQ

Utlas Inc
EASTWIND
INFOQUEST
INNOVACQ

Visicorp
VISILINK

Vista System Ltd
VIDEO LIBRARY SYSTEM

Westminster Medical Systems Ltd
MEDICAL LIBRARIAN

Winnebago Software Co
CATALOG CARD MAKER III
COMPUTER CAT : MULTI USER
LIBRARY CIRCULATION SYSTEM II
LIBRARY CIRCULATION SYSTEM III